Mike Meyers' A+® Guide to PC Hardware Lab Manual

Michael Meyers
Lloyd Jeffries

McGraw-Hill Technology Education

New York Chicago San Francisco Lisbon London Madrid Mexico City Milan
New Delhi San Juan Seoul Singapore Sydney Toronto

1333 Burr Ridge Parkway
Burr Ridge, Illinois 60527
U.S.A.

Mike Meyers' A+® Guide to PC Hardware Lab Manual

For information on translations or book distributors outside the U.S.A., please see the International Contact Information page immediately following the index of this book. Some ancillaries, including electronic and print components, may not be available to customers outside the United States.

1 2 3 4 5 6 7 8 9 0 QPD QPD 0 1 9 8 7 6 5 4

ISBN 0-07-223122-X

This book was composed with QuarkXPress 4.11 on a Macintosh G4.

www.mhteched.com

Sponsoring Editor
Christopher Johnson

Developmental Editor
Pamela Woolf

IT Skills Consultant
Laurie Stephan

Project Editor
Laurie Stewart
Happenstance Type-O-Rama

Copy Editor
Kim Wimpsett

Proofreader
Paul Medoff

Indexer
Jack Lewis

Composition
Craig Woods
Happenstance Type-O-Rama

Illustrator
Jeffrey Wilson
Happenstance Type-O-Rama

Series Design
Maureen Forys
Happenstance Type-O-Rama

Cover Series Design
Jeff Weeks

Cover Photograph
Tom Collicott/Masterfile

Mike Meyers' A+® Guide to PC Hardware Lab Manual

To Sue Leanox, for teaching me how to keep the smoke in the chips.

—Mike Meyers

I dedicate this book to my wife, Raylene. She is very patient and understands my need to immerse myself in the realm of computer repair and to teach others to become excellent technicians focused on user needs. She is always there with the barley green and vitamins to keep me going.

—Lloyd Jeffries

About the Authors

Michael Meyers is the industry's leading authority on A+ Certification. He is the president and co-founder of Total Seminars, LLC, a provider of PC and network repair seminars, books, videos, and courseware for thousands of organizations throughout the world. Mike has been involved in the computer and network repair industry since 1977 as a technician, instructor, author, consultant, and speaker. Author of numerous popular PC books and A+ and Network+ courseware, Mike is also the Series Editor for both the highly successful *Mike Meyers' Certification Passport* series and the *Mike Meyers' Computer Skills* series, both published by McGraw-Hill/Osborne. Mike holds multiple industry certifications and considers the moniker "computer nerd" a compliment.

Lloyd Jeffries came to Total Seminars after 31 years of customer service with NCR Corp. While at NCR, in addition to holding various management positions, he spent 20 years as a field technician and six years as a technical trainer, becoming an accredited course developer. His CBT course on computer number systems for NCR field technicians was also sold to the general public. At Total Seminars, he teaches CompTIA certification courses and manages other instructors. Lloyd's CompTIA certifications include A+, Network+, Server+ and iNet+.

About the Technical Editor

Lee Cottrell has been teaching computer programming, hardware and networking at the Bradford School in Pittsburgh, Pennsylvania, for more than ten years. In addition to his teaching duties, Lee maintains the school's LANs and computers. He holds an MS degree in Information Science from the University of Pittsburgh. Lee has authored and contributed to several books from the McGraw-Hill/Osborne line.

Contents

Acknowledgments

This book was a highly collaborative effort, and in this case, top collaborator honors go to Total Seminars CEO, Dudley Lehmer, who labored tirelessly over virtually every aspect of the project, even taking up an editing pen, to make sure it would be a success.

David Biggs did his usual superlative graphics work on an extremely tight schedule, as well as contributing to the writing and editing process. The A+ expertise and technical writing skills of Martin Acuña and Scott Jernigan were brought to bear with great effect on almost every chapter, ensuring that the final product was accurate, up to date, and educationally sound.

Scott, Martin, and David were ably assisted in their work by Total Seminars' crack editors Cary Dier and Cindy Clayton, as well as Jeremy Conn, our "Grow Your Own Geek Authors" project guinea pig.

Special thanks go to one of Lloyd's instructors, Lida Kafka, for her creative suggestions and valuable feedback.

As always, the folks at McGraw-Hill kept the train on the tracks and our noses to the grindstone. Chris Johnson's velvet-clad fist of iron kept us moving and "near" deadline. Pamela Woolf provided her usual superlative support as the project's developmental editor, and Laurie Stewart's Happenstance Type-O-Rama team wielded its copy editor's red pen and compositor's pica ruler with great effectiveness.

Preface

Information Technology Skill Standards and Your Curriculum

Students in today's increasingly competitive IT career market are differentiated not only by their technical skills, but by their communication, problem solving, and teaming skills. More and more, these professional skills are the ones that guarantee career longevity and success. The National Workforce Center for Emerging Technologies (NWCET) and McGraw-Hill Technology Education have partnered in an effort to help you build technical *and* employability skills in the classroom.

NWCET and McGraw-Hill in Partnership

McGraw-Hill Technology Education and the NWCET have partnered with the goal of helping IT educators by making the IT skill standards more easily available and ready to use. McGraw-Hill Technology Education and the NWCET have developed four different products that will help you address the IT skill standards in your A+ programs and courses:

- A summary crosswalk that highlights the IT skill standards addressed by the McGraw-Hill *Mike Meyers' A+ Guide to PC Hardware*.

- A detailed crosswalk listing Technical Knowledge, Employability Skills, and Performance Indicators addressed by the compliant curriculum (textbook, lab manual, and learning activities in the instructor pack CD).

- 16 skill standards–based activities with associated assessment tools.

- A training document that helps instructors understand and use the features of teaching a skill standards–aligned curriculum.

These four products give you a very solid basis on which to deliver skill standards–based curriculum to your students. They are explained in some detail here:

Summary crosswalk Maps the content of the A+ textbook to the NWCET IT skill standards. The crosswalk is provided in Table 1. Each chapter is listed with the correlated key activity performed by a technical support person as these have been identified in the industry as the skill standards. For instance, Chapter 1 correlates closely to Key Activity C2—Evaluate present data and system configuration. The following list will help you demonstrate to your stakeholders that your curriculum maps to industry-identified workplace skills. It will also help you focus on which workplace skills are most emphasized in your curriculum.

Chapter	Key Activity
Chapter 1	C2: Evaluate present data and system configuration
Chapter 2	C4: Install, configure, and test system hardware and peripherals
Chapter 3	C4: Install, configure, and test system hardware and peripherals
Chapter 4	C2: Evaluate present data and system configuration
Chapter 5	C4: Install, configure, and test system hardware and peripherals
Chapter 6	C4: Install, configure, and test system hardware and peripherals
Chapter 7	D1: Operate computer system and run system applications
Chapter 8	C4: Install, configure, and test system hardware and peripherals
Chapter 9	C4: Install, configure, and test system hardware and peripherals
Chapter 10	C4: Install, configure, and test system hardware and peripherals
Chapter 11	C4: Install, configure, and test system hardware and peripherals
Chapter 12	C4: Install, configure, and test system hardware and peripherals
Chapter 13	C4: Install, configure, and test system hardware and peripherals
Chapter 14	C2: Evaluate present data and system configuration
Chapter 15	C4: Install, configure, and test system hardware and peripherals
Chapter 16	C2: Evaluate present data and system configuration

TABLE 1 Summary Crosswalk

Detailed crosswalk Illustrates how each chapter of the textbook, the lab manual, and the NWCET-developed supplemental learning activities on the instructor CD map to the IT skill standards. An excerpt of this crosswalk is provided in Table 2. This matrix maps out all your resources and provides you with sound learning outcomes and performance assessment criteria for your curriculum. This detailed crosswalk illustrates how a skill standards–compliant curriculum emphasizes both technical and employability skills. For instance, in Chapter 2, the supplemental activity requires students to write a memo to be distributed to all technicians within a fictitious company explaining the procedure for avoiding ESD incidences. An assessment rubric to grade student memos is provided and is based on the performance indicators in the crosswalk that focus on skills like documentation and organization of information.

Learning activities Mapped to the IT skill standards and include learning outcomes, student handouts, and rubrics for assessment. There are 16 learning activities on the instructor CD.

Training document Provides you with background information about the NWCET IT skill standards, how they're developed, and how they're used within industry and education.

Mike Meyers' A+ Guide to PC Hardware Chapter and Instructor Pack CD Activity	Learning Outcomes (students will be able to)	NWCET IT Skill Standards (Critical Function and Key Activity)	NWCET IT Skill Standards Technical Knowledge	NWCET IT Skill Standards Employability Skills	NWCET IT Skill Standards Performance Indicators
Chapter 1: Visible PC	Describe how the PC works	**Critical Work Functions**	Ability to identify system components	Ability to understand, interpret and recognize the accuracy of information	Information is effectively and correctly gathered, organized and analyzed
Instructor Pack CD Activity 1: Memo Regarding ESD Incidents	Identify the essential tools of the trade and avoid electrostatic discharge	C: Perform Hardware and Software Installation, Configuration and Upgrades	Knowledge of technical terms		Documentation is clear and accurate
	Identify the major internal and external components of a PC	A: Perform Troubleshooting		Ability to use appropriate language and terminology	Hardware and software problems are clearly identified
	Identify the different connectors on a typical PC system unit	**Key Activities**		Ability to accurately summarize and document information	Resolutions are documented to the appropriate level of detail
	Document procedures for avoiding ESD activity	C2: Evaluate present data and system configuration		Ability to organize and present technical information in a logical and consistent manner	
		A7: Document hardware and software problems and resolutions			

TABLE 2 An Example of the Detailed Crosswalk

NWCET Background and Mission

In 1995, the National Science Foundation (NSF) designated and funded the NWCET as a National Center of Excellence in Advanced Technological Education. The Center was created to advance Information Technology (IT) education and improve the supply, quality, and diversity of the IT workforce.

The National Workforce Center for Emerging Technologies has since become a leader in new designs for IT education, developing products, services, and best practices that provide timely, relevant, and lasting solutions to meet the needs of IT educators and the IT workforce. The NWCET translates the rapidly changing demands of the technology workplace into programs, curricula, courseware, and assessments that prepare students for current and future IT careers.

The NWCET is perhaps best known for its IT skill standards. Skill standards provide an agreement of what is expected to be successful in a given career area. They provide a validated, industry-derived framework upon which educators can build curricula. Using industry skill standards as the foundation for curricula will result in a closer alignment between educational programs and workplace expectations, and result in a better-skilled workforce. To support new and innovative IT programs and degrees, the NWCET (www.nwcet.org) provides other professional development opportunities for high school teachers and community college and university faculty. The Educator-to-Educator Institute (E2E) (http://e2e.nwcet.org), the training branch of the NWCET, is dedicated to helping IT educators achieve excellence in IT instruction. CyberCareers (www.cybercareers.org) is a web site oriented toward middle and high school students and teachers, providing a wide variety of career education materials such as job descriptions and an IT Interest Inventory.

Instructor and Student Web Site

For instructor and student resources, check out www.mikemeyersaplus.com or mhteched.com. You'll find all sorts of stuff that will help you learn more about troubleshooting and fixing computers.

Additional Resources for Teachers

Resources for teachers are provided via an instructor's resource kit that maps to the organization of *Mike Meyers' A+ Guide to PC Hardware* and includes solutions to exercises in the lab manual. This instructor's resource kit includes the following:

- Answer keys to the end-of-chapter activities in the textbook and solutions in the lab manual

- ExamView® Pro testbank software that generates a wide array of paper- or network-based tests, and features automatic grading

- Thousands of questions, written by experienced IT instructors

- A wide variety of question types and difficulty levels, allowing teachers to customize each test to maximize student progress

- Engaging PowerPoint slides on the lecture topics

- WebCT and Blackboard cartridges

Chapter 1

The Visible PC

Lab Exercises

Every competent tech knows the PC inside and out. Nothing destroys your credibility in the eyes of a client as quickly as not knowing the basics, like the difference between the power and reset buttons. "Oops!" doesn't always go over well in the real world! This set of labs applies the information you learned in Chapter 1 of the *Mike Meyers' A+ Guide to PC Hardware*, and has you poking and prodding a PC. We'll start with typical user-accessible components, then examine the connectors found on most PCs, and finish up with a tour inside the case.

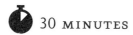 30 MINUTES

Lab Exercise 1.01: Examining User-Accessible Components

It's been one of those days. You've walked into what should have been a simple job interview only to meet a very frantic IT manager who's dealing with a crisis of *epic* proportions. She doesn't even bother to interview you, but hands you a boot disk and a CD-ROM filled with utilities and says, "Go check Jane's PC, fourth cubicle on the left. Don't change anything or open it up. Right now I simply need to know if it'll boot properly and access the drives." And then she's off to deal with her crisis and you're on the spot.

This exercise looks at the many components that a user can access without removing the case. You can use a quick scan such as this to determine whether a PC is functioning properly at the most basic level. Take your time and jot down notes where you feel the need. Practice each step until you are confident you can do it on the job as a PC tech.

Learning Objectives

In this lab exercise you'll locate and describe the various cabinet parts, user controls, and built-in user-accessible devices of a PC system. You'll not remove the system cover during this lab.

At the end of this lab, you'll be able to

- Recognize and manipulate user controls

- Describe how to use user-accessible devices

Lab Materials and Setup

The materials you need for this lab are

- One fully functioning desktop computer system unit capable of booting from a floppy disk, with a working CD- or DVD-media drive

- One Windows 98 second edition (SE) bootable floppy disk

✔ **Hint**

If you don't have a Windows 98 SE boot disk, you can make one by following this procedure: Insert a known good (not physically damaged) floppy disk into the floppy drive of a system running Windows 98 SE. Using the mouse, select Start | Settings | Control Panel, and then double-click the Add/Remove Programs icon. Locate the Startup Disk tab at the top and click it. Now click Create Disk.

- One readable data CD-ROM containing files

- One keyboard

- One mouse

- One printer (optional)

- A notepad on which to take notes and sketch the computer and components

✔ **Hint**

Get used to taking notes and drawing pictures. Even today after 40 years of repairing computers from mainframes to PCs, I still use a notepad to keep track of what I see and what I change. I suggest you save your drawings and notes, as you may find them useful in subsequent labs.

Getting Down to Business

As a technician, you need to know how everything works on a PC. The best place to begin is with the externally accessible devices.

Step 1 Before you can do much work with a PC, you need a functioning output device, such as a monitor. Check the monitor to see if it has power. The small LED on or near the monitor's power button should be lit: orange if the system is turned off or asleep; green if the system is fully on. If you determine that the monitor is not plugged into the wall, do so now.

Figure 1-1 Recognizing the On/Off and Reset buttons on the front of a PC

Step 2   Look at the front of your system unit. Locate the On/Off button and the reset switch. Compare your buttons to the ones in Figure 1-1.

Once you have located the On/Off button or switch on your system, make a note of its appearance. Is it in plain sight, or hidden behind a door or lid? Is it round, square, or some odd shape? Did you know that pressing the On button to start a PC when the electricity is off is known as a *cold boot* or sometimes a hard boot?

Describe your On/Off switch here.

_____

Now locate the Reset button. It is normally near the On/Off button and much smaller in size. Some systems even have the button recessed into the case so it is hard to press accidentally. (Don't panic if there is no Reset button—not all systems have them.) Sometimes software will lock up the system, and the only way to restart without turning off the power is by pressing the Reset switch.

One other observation: notice the two LEDs on the front panel near the On/Off button. One will generally light up green to indicate the power is on, and the other will flash red when the internal hard drive is active.

✔ **Hint**

On older systems the On/Off button or switch may be located on the back of the system. Some newer systems have an On/Off switch located on the back that controls the flow of electricity to the power supply, and an On/Off button on the front that boots and shuts down the PC.

Step 3 Now locate the floppy drive. You can recognize it by its 3.5-inch horizontal slot. Do you see the eject button below the slot on the right side of the drive? Below the slot on the left side is a light emitting diode (LED). It lights up when the drive is actively reading or writing information on a floppy disk.

Your system should also have a tray that will open to accept the insertion of a CD or DVD disc. Locate the CD- or DVD-media drive on your system. It too has a button in the lower-right corner. When the system is on, you can press that button to open the tray door, and the tray will slide out to receive your disc (see Figure 1-2). Pressing the button while the tray is out will make the tray retract back into the drive so it can read the disc.

✖ Warning

Do not force the CD or DVD tray to close. Always press the button on the front of the drive to close the tray or to eject a disc. Forcing the tray to close can cause the gears inside to become misaligned, so the tray will not close properly.

✔ Hint

If you forget to remove a CD or DVD disc before turning off the power, you can straighten a strong paper clip and insert it into the tiny hole on the front of the CD- or DVD-media drive. Pressing straight inward with the paper clip will cause the tray to open.

Figure 1-2 Can you locate the floppy drive and CD-ROM drive on this unit?

Your system may have other devices installed such as Zip drives, tape drives, or media card slots, such as those for Compact Flash or Memory Stick cards. Each of these use removable media, and you must take care when inserting or removing the media.

Step 4   Make sure your system is completely off. Insert the bootable Windows 98 SE floppy disk into the floppy drive, and press the On button located on the front of the PC. As the system boots up, it will stop and display the Windows 98 Startup menu. Select option 1, Start Computer with CD-ROM Support. The system will display lines of text on the monitor for a minute or two more as it loads software.

✖ Warning

Depending on the software currently installed on the hard drive in your system, you may encounter some hard drive error messages when you boot using the Windows 98 floppy disk. Such messages could appear if a different operating system, such as Windows NT, Windows 2000/XP, or Linux, has prepared the hard drive in a format not compatible with Windows 98 SE. For purposes of this lab, you can ignore these messages about the hard drive. If the system doesn't seem to know it has a floppy drive, the problem may be that the floppy drive has been disabled in the CMOS setup utility (see Lab Exercise 9.02). You'll have to fix this before you can continue with this lab.

Describe here the contents of the last two lines of text displayed on the monitor.

_____

_____

Step 5   Now press the reset button and watch the system monitor.

What appears on the screen this time? _____

Are the last three lines of text the same as those you noted previously? _____

Step 6   Press the eject button on the front of the CD- or DVD-media drive, and when the tray opens, carefully insert a CD-ROM. Press the eject button again to close the tray. Practice inserting and removing a CD-ROM until you feel comfortable with the process. Did the LED on the front of the CD-ROM drive flash or stay on continuously during your practice? _____

Step 7   Pretend you lost power and must remove the CD from the drive without power. Use a paper clip as noted in the previous Hint to remove the CD.

Turn off the system by pressing the On/Off button. If the power does not turn off right away, press and hold the button for five to ten seconds until it does turn off.

Step 8   As a technician you need to understand the keyboard, because it is still one of the most important human interfaces on a PC. Look at the way your keyboard is laid out. It basically has three main sections with some extra keys. For the most part it has a standard classic QWERTY (pronounced "KWERTY")
keyboard layout familiar to touch typists everywhere. Those of you who never took typing may be wonder-
ing, "What's QWERTY?" Keyboards got that name because those are the first six letters in the top row of
letter keys (see Figure 1-3).

To the right of the main keyboard there is a square numeric keypad like you find on old adding
machines. This feature is beloved by people like accountants or merchants who must work on long
columns of figures because with practice you can input numbers really quickly that way.

Above the rows of letter and number keys on the keyboard you'll find a special row of (often
smaller-sized) keys called function keys, normally labeled F1 through F12 (see Figure 1-3). What these
keys do depends on the software you are using when you press them. Pressing the F1 key often calls up
the program's Help feature; other keys might work as shortcuts for performing specific tasks, insert
some type of data into the program, or even modify the way the system starts up. You'll use function
keys a lot when you troubleshoot systems.

Look at the very top-left corner of the keyboard next to the function keys and find the ESC key. In
many programs, particularly older ones, pressing this "Escape" key (that really is what ESC stands for)
backs you up a step (sort of an "Oops, didn't mean to do that!" key), or even exits the program. In more
modern software, pressing ESC will often make the program "let go of" some text or graphic you
selected, or end some mode or feature you started up by mistake.

Figure 1-3 Exploring the QWERTY keyboard

To the right of the function keys are the PRINT SCREEN (PRTSCN), SCROLL LOCK (SCRLK), and PAUSE/BREAK keys. These specialized keys aren't much used anymore, although some programs utilize the PRTSCN key to capture snapshots of whatever's showing on the monitor.

Along the bottom row of the keyboard you'll find the special keys labeled CTRL (control) and ALT (alternate), and on some Microsoft keyboards you'll also find a key with a Windows symbol, and one with a menu symbol. For the most part, the CTRL and ALT keys don't do anything by themselves, but they are incredibly useful when combined with other keys. In many word processing programs, for example, holding down the CTRL key while pressing the S key has the same effect as selecting File | Save using the mouse—but faster and easier. Techs use these types of key combinations a lot. (The standard shorthand for writing a key combination is to hyphenate the special key and the character key, so to stay with our example, the Save shortcut is written CTRL-S.)

 30 MINUTES

Lab Exercise 1.02: Recognizing External Connections

Just as you finish working with Jane's PC, her intercom buzzes. It's the head of IT and she's got a new assignment for you: The new satellite office in Albuquerque has gotten a delivery of new PCs, but the machines are all in boxes and not one of the sales people there knows a mouse from a monkey wrench. Your job is to call them up and walk them through the process of connecting a PC, describing each cable and connector, and explaining how they connect to the PC.

Learning Objectives

In this lab, you'll identify, describe, and explain the functions of the external connections on a standard PC.

At the end of this lab, you'll be able to

- Identify the external connectors on a PC and the related cables

- Explain the function of each external connection

Lab Materials and Setup

The materials you need for this lab are

- A study partner, if possible (or this lab can be done alone)

- At least one fully-functioning PC computer system less than two years old (two or more systems is ideal, with one older and one newer than two years old)

- A notepad on which to take notes and sketch the computer and components

✔ **Cross-Reference**

Before you begin this lab, read the "Connectors" and "All Kinds of Connectors" sections in Chapter 1 of *Mike Meyers' A+ Guide to PC Hardware*.

✔ **Hint**

If this is the same computer you used in the previous lab and if you saved your drawings and notes, you may reuse those drawings and notes in this lab.

Getting Down to Business

It is time to learn about all the external things that can be attached to a PC. This lab will step you through identifying and understanding the function of these connectors.

✖ **Warning**

Shut off the power to your system and unplug your PC from the wall socket before doing the following exercise.

✔ **Hint**

Cables have conductors. A conductor is a wire that can carry electrical signals. You sometimes describe a cable by the number of conductors it has. For example, a telephone cable can be a two- or four-conductor cable. A power cable is a three-conductor cable. A network cable is an eight-conductor cable.

Step 1   Look at all those wires coming from the back of your PC. There is a power cable, a telephone cable, a printer cable, a keyboard cable, a mouse cable, and the list goes on and on depending on your system. Looking at the back of my current system (the one I'm using to write this manual), I count 15 cables directly connected to it.

The great thing about PCs is it is difficult to connect the cables incorrectly. Each one has a unique connector. Some will be male (connectors with pins), and some will be female (connectors with holes). Each connector has a particular shape and a specific number of pins or holes that match those of a specific device connected to the system unit.

Get your notepad ready to take notes and draw pictures.

Step 2   Unplug each of your PC's cables one at a time and practice plugging it back in until you get a feel for how it fits. How is each cable held in place and prevented from coming loose? Is there a screw, clip, or some other fastener that holds the cable connector tight to the system? What does it connect to? What is the shape of the connector on each end? Is it round, rectangular, D-shaped? How many pins or holes does it have? How many rows of pins or holes?

Step 3   Is it possible to plug any of the cables into the wrong connector? If so, which one(s)? What do you think would happen?

_____

_____

Step 4   Remove or disconnect any of the following cables from your system and describe its connector. Follow this example:

- Data cable from the monitor to the PC

    Type of connector: End 1 (PC) <u>DB</u>   End 2 <u>DB</u>

    Male or female: End 1 (PC) <u>F</u>   End 2 <u>M</u>

    Number of pins/holes/conductors: 15

✔ **Hint**

Your PC may not have all these cables! That's okay!

Now it's your turn:

- Data cable from the printer to the PC (both ends)

    Type of connector: End 1 (PC) _____ End 2 _____

    Male or Female: End 1 (PC) _____ End 2 _____

    Number of pins/holes/conductors: _____

- Data cable from the keyboard to the PC

    Type of connector: End 1 (PC) _____ End 2 _____

    Male or Female: End 1 (PC) _____ End 2 _____

    Number of pins/holes/conductors: _____

- Data cable from the mouse to the PC

     Type of connector: End 1 (PC) _____ End 2 _____

     Male or Female: End 1 (PC) _____ End 2 _____

     Number of pins/holes/conductors: _____

- Data cable from the network to the PC

     Type of connector: End 1 (PC) _____ End 2 _____

     Male or Female: End 1 (PC) _____ End 2 _____

     Number of pins/holes/conductors: _____

- Data cable (telephone wire) from the internal modem to the telephone wall jack

     Type of connector: End 1 (PC) _____ End 2 _____

     Male or Female: End 1 (PC) _____ End 2 _____

     Number of pins/holes/conductors: _____

Step 5   Reconnect all the cables properly and prepare to turn on the system. If you have an On/Off button on the back of the system, flip it on. Make sure the monitor is turned on.

Step 6   If you're working with someone else, play "Flash Cords." Have your partner hold up various cables. Try to guess what they connect to by the connectors on the ends. Then switch roles with your partner.

Step 7   Examine other computers to see if they have different connectors than the ones you have been working with. See if you can identify the peripherals that connect to those sockets and plugs.

Step 8   The two system units in Figure 1-4 look different, but they have many connectors in common. Try to find the following connectors on each system unit:

- Power
- Monitor
- Mouse
- Keyboard
- Printer
- Network

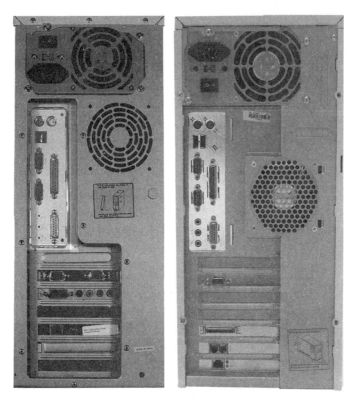

FIGURE 1-4 Can you match the connectors on these two system units?

Step 9 Describe the connector that matches each type of cable in the list. Use Chapter 1 of *Mike Meyers' A+ Guide to PC Hardware* or your notes for reference.

Cable Type	Connector Type(s)
Keyboard cable	_____
Mouse cable	_____
Speaker cable	_____
Monitor data cable	_____
Printer data cable (printer end)	_____
Printer data cable (PC end)	_____
Network data cable	_____
Modem/telephone wire	_____

Step 10 Identify the following connectors. What is the name of each connector, and what does it connect to?

A. _____

B. _____

C. _____

D. _____

E. _____

F. _____

G. _____

H. _____

I. _____

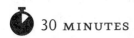

30 MINUTES

Lab Exercise 1.03: Recognizing Internal Components and Connections

When you're on the job, you'll encounter different models of personal computers manufactured by different companies. After you open a computer case, you should be able to identify the major internal parts of the PC system, regardless of the manufacturer. This lab exercise will help you practice doing that.

As promised, it's now time to go under the hood.

Learning Objectives

In this lab exercise you'll locate and describe the various internal components and connectors of a standard PC system.

At the end of this lab, you'll be able to

- Recognize all major components inside a PC

- Name the function of each component

- Understand the relationship of internal components to external connections

Lab Materials and Setup

The materials you need for this lab are

- One fully functioning PC system

- Thermal paste to reattach the CPU fan to the CPU

- A notepad on which to take notes and sketch the computer and components

Getting Down to Business

In the previous lab you examined the external connectors and cables; now it is time to look inside.

✖ Warning

Shut off the power to your system and unplug your PC from the wall socket before doing the following exercise.

Step 1   Disconnect all the external cables (monitor, keyboard, mouse, printer, and so on) from the PC you are going to use and place it on a flat, stable surface (preferably on a static pad) where you can sit or stand comfortably to inspect the insides.

Step 2   Use proper electrostatic discharge (ESD) procedures while opening the case and during this entire exercise. Take the cover off your system, using either a large Phillips screwdriver or a hex driver to remove the retaining screws, and then lay the computer down so the open side faces the ceiling.

✔ Cross-Reference

Review Chapter 1 of *Mike Meyers' A+ Guide to PC Hardware* to confirm your understanding of proper ESD procedures, and how to open a PC system case.

Look inside your PC system case. What do you see? To begin with, you'll see lots of cables and wires. Some appear to be single-colored wires, and others seem to be multiple gray-colored wires in the shape of wide ribbons. Most colored wires originate at the power supply and end at the various devices to supply the needed direct current (DC) power to run the PC. The wide ribbon cables attach between devices to transfer data. These ribbon cables are sometimes referred to as *logic cables* or *data cables*.

See if you can locate in your system case the major components labeled in Figure 1-5. You may have to move some of the wires and cables in order to find them, especially components on the motherboard, but remember your ESD procedures and be gentle. Sometimes the slightest bump is enough to unseat a connection.

Step 3   Look in your PC and see if you can locate the CPU. Running CPUs generate quite a bit of heat, so they need their own dedicated cooling mechanisms. Therefore, if you're looking at a working system, the CPU will be hiding under a fan/heatsink unit. If you're allowed to do so, *carefully* remove and then reattach the fan unit. Remember that before reattaching it, you must apply a thin film of thermal paste to the underside of the fan where it contacts the CPU. Do not remove the CPU at this time.

> ✖ **Warning**
>
> Make sure you fully understand how to remove your particular model of CPU fan before you try it!

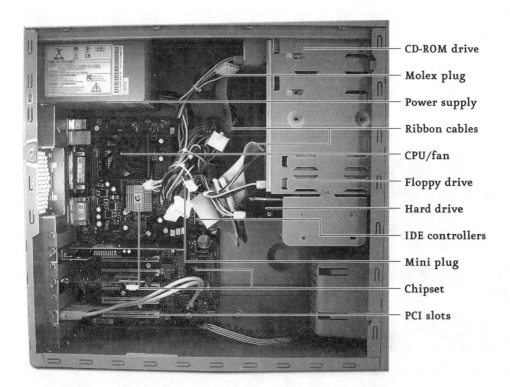

Figure 1-5 Inside a typical PC

Make a note of the type of chip you have (if you removed the fan).

If you're in a computer lab with multiple systems, examine a number of different CPU chips. Take notice of where each CPU is located on its motherboard.

Step 4   Look in your PC and find the random access memory (RAM) modules. RAM comes in thin wafer-like modules, about three to five inches long by one inch wide. A row of metal contacts running along one of the long edges plugs into a matching three- to five-inch long socket on the motherboard. Look for a long wafer standing on edge; often you'll find two or more RAM modules lined up in a row.

How many RAM modules do you have? _____

Do you have Dual Inline Memory Modules (DIMMs) or Single Inline Memory Modules (SIMMs)?

_____

Again, if possible, look at several different PCs, preferably both older and newer models.

Step 5   Now look in your PC and find the expansion slots. How many expansion cards can be plugged into your system? _____ Some of the expansion slots may have cards in them. These may be modem cards, sound cards, network cards, and video cards.

Look at the expansion cards installed in your PC, and then look at the external connectors on each. Can you match the cable to the expansion card?

Step 6   Locate the large silver box mounted next to the back panel of the case. It is the power supply.

Trace the colored wires leading out of it. Remember to be *gentle*.

Find the power plug(s) for the motherboard. Does it look like the one in Figure 1-6? If you have a newer PC, it probably will. If you have an older PC, it might not because some older motherboards use a pair of power connectors.

FIGURE 1-6 P1 power connector and matching motherboard socket

FIGURE 1-7 Investigating power connectors

Find the power connectors for the floppy drive, CD- or DVD-media drive (if there is one), and hard drive(s). Do they look like one of the connectors in Figure 1-7? They should!

Step 7   Now look at the floppy drive. It should have a flat ribbon cable attached to it.

Trace the cable to the motherboard. If you can, do this on several computers. Do the same for the hard drive(s) and for the CD or DVD drive, if present.

These cables are about 1.5 inches wide, and they are usually gray with a colored stripe on one side. The stripe—usually red—orients the cable properly to the connections on the motherboard and the drive.

The cable to the floppy drive has 34 wires (conductors), and in many cases has a twist in the center. Its position relative to this seven-wire twist determines whether a floppy drive is the primary or A: drive (attached to the connector at the end of the cable past the twist), or the secondary B: drive (on the center connector).

✔ **Hint**

It's rare to find two floppy drives in a newer system, and manufacturers may use a shorter floppy cable with no twist and no second drive connector.

The flat ribbon cable that connects most hard drive(s) and CD- or DVD-media drives to the motherboard has 40 wires and no twist. You may even have a newer cable of 80 conductors to allow for faster transmission of the data to and from the hard drives. Both cables still have a different-colored edge on one side for orientation, however. Many current systems have a much smaller, seven-wire cable for the hard drive that has connectors keyed like the letter L.

Step 8   After noting the current state of the ribbon cables, disconnect and reconnect each device's cable in turn. Practice this a few times. Will the cable go on backward? Try it. Put the cable on the device backward if you can. Older-style cables can be put on incorrectly. Newer cables and connectors have built-in keying to prevent this from happening. Make sure the cables are properly connected when you've finished.

Look at where the ribbon cables connect to the motherboard. Make note of the proper cable orientation. Practice disconnecting and reconnecting the cables to the motherboard. Do you have any problems if you try to connect these backward?

Step 9   See if you can locate any jumpers or DIP switches on your motherboard. Resist the temptation to play with them at this point—just make a note of what you find. In particular, look for the identifying labels on the motherboard.

Step 10   Identify the components in Figure 1-8.

A. _____   F. _____

B. _____   G. _____

C. _____   H. _____

D. _____   I. _____

E. _____

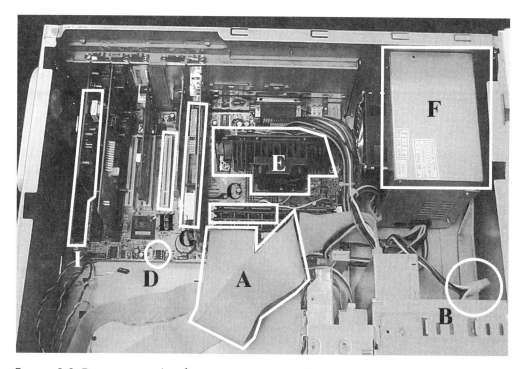

FIGURE 1-8 Do you recognize these components inside your PC?

Lab Analysis Test

1. Joe has just moved his PC to his new office. After hooking up all the cables, he turns on the system. When it asks for his password, the keyboard will not respond. What could possibly be wrong?

_____

_____

2. Teresa has an older PC system and notices that every time she adjusts the position of the monitor on her desk the colors on the display go berserk and then correct themselves. Why?

_____

_____

3. Cal has purchased a new set of speakers for his PC. The old ones worked just fine, but he wanted more power and a subwoofer. When he plugged in the new speakers, they would not work. Power is on to the speakers. What is the first thing you would check?

_____

_____

4. John had a new modem installed in his computer at a local mom-and-pop shop, where he watched as the system successfully connected to his AOL account. When he got home and tried, however, he couldn't get a dial tone. He calls you to ask for help. What should you suggest that he check first?

_____

_____

5. Raylene removed the case of her PC to determine what type of RAM she has installed. When she put the case back on and tried to start the PC, she got a message that there's a problem with her hard drive. What is a good reason this might have happened?

_____

_____

Key Term Quiz

Use the following vocabulary terms to complete the following sentences. Not all of the terms will be used.

ALT key

CTRL key

data cable

female connector

function key

LED

male connector

power cable

Windows 98 boot disk

1. The _____ for a floppy drive is a 34-pin ribbon cable.

2. When a floppy or CD/DVD drive is being accessed, a(n) _____ on the face of the drive lights up.

3. A keyboard shortcut for saving a document is to press the _____ in combination with the s key.

4. A _____ has pins, while a _____ has holes.

5. Pressing the FI _____ often calls up a program's Help feature.

Chapter 2

Microprocessors

Lab Exercises

Many PC users are comfortable performing the simpler installation and upgrade tasks, such as adding RAM or installing a modem or sound card. When it comes to the more complicated tasks, however, such as installing or replacing a *central processing unit* (CPU), wise users turn to the experts—this means *you*!

Installing a CPU is one of the many "bread-and-butter" tasks that you'll find yourself performing over and over as a PC tech. Whether you're building a new system from scratch or replacing the CPU on an existing computer, it's your job to know the important characteristics of the CPU, match the CPU to compatible motherboards, and configure the CPU on the PC.

In this set of lab exercises, you'll identify current CPU types, form factors, sockets, and slots, and practice installing a CPU/fan assembly on a motherboard. Let's get started.

 30 MINUTES

Lab Exercise 2.01: CPU Characteristics

There you are, innocently strolling down the hall at work, following the smell of freshly brewed coffee, when you're ambushed by Joe the accountant, brandishing a CPU/fan unit. He wants to replace the CPU in his machine with this new one he bought on eBay, and he wants you to help him. When you're the resident computer tech geek, your coworkers will expect you to be able to deal knowledgably with a situation like Joe's.

Staying on top of the many developments in CPU technology can be challenging, but it's also a necessary part of your job as a PC technician. By this point, you know that you can't just plug any CPU into any motherboard and expect it to work: you have to match the *right* CPU to the *right* motherboard. To accomplish this, you need to identify important CPU characteristics such as form factor, clock speed, and bus speed, as well as things like voltage settings, clock multiplier configurations, and cooling requirements.

Learning Objectives

In this lab, you'll practice identifying CPUs and CPU fan components.

At the end of this lab, you'll be able to

- Recognize the different kinds of CPUs

- Recognize different CPU fan attachments

- Identify the basic features of different classes of CPUs

Lab Materials and Setup

The materials you need for this lab are

- One desktop computer system

- One anti-static mat

- A notepad

✖ Warning

This exercise requires you to remove the PC case cover. Remember to follow proper electrostatic discharge (ESD) procedures to avoid damaging any components.

Getting Down to Business

In the following steps, you'll review your knowledge of CPU specifications, and then examine the CPU and fan attachment of a PC.

✔ Cross-Reference

Use Chapter 2 of *Mike Meyers' A+ Guide to PC Hardware* to help fill in the numbers for each CPU in the following charts.

✔ Hint

Another source of CPU information is the CPU manufacturer. Look at the documentation that came with your PC or CPU for the important specifications, or check the maker's web site. There, you'll find full descriptions of the CPU's package type, frontside bus speed, cache size, clock multiplier, and so on.

Step 1 For your first exercise, fill in the size of the external data bus (EDB) and address bus in the chart for all the listed CPUs.

CPU	External Data Bus Bits	Address Bus Bits
Intel Pentium	_____	_____
Intel Pentium Pro	_____	_____
Intel Celeron	_____	_____
Intel Pentium III	_____	_____
Intel Pentium 4	_____	_____
Intel Pentium II Xeon	_____	_____
Intel Pentium III Xeon	_____	_____
Intel Pentium 4 Xeon	_____	_____
Intel Itanium	_____	_____
Intel Itanium II	_____	_____
AMD Athlon	_____	_____
AMD Duron	_____	_____
AMD Athlon XP	_____	_____
AMD Opteron	_____	_____

Step 2 See how many of the chip features you can fill in knowing the maker and CPU type:

	Maker	CPU Type	Package	MB Bus Speed (MHz)	Cache L1 (KB)	L2 (KB)	Clock Speed Multiplier
A	Intel	Pentium III 750	_____	_____	_____	_____	_____
B	AMD	Athlon 600	_____	_____	_____	_____	_____
C	AMD	Duron 800	_____	_____	_____	_____	_____
D	Intel	Celeron 566	_____	_____	_____	_____	_____
E	AMD	K6-2 475	_____	_____	_____	_____	_____
F	Intel	Pentium II 450	_____	_____	_____	_____	_____
G	Intel	Pentium 4 1300	_____	_____	_____	_____	_____
H	Intel	Pentium 4 Xeon	_____	_____	_____	_____	_____
I	Intel	Itanium	_____	_____	_____	_____	_____

Figure 2-1 Exploring different CPUs

Step 3 Look at the chips pictured in Figure 2-1, making note of the differences you see. In particular, look for

- Package types: Pin Grid Array (PGA) or Single Edge Contact Cartridge (SEC)
- Pin arrays
- Orientation guide notches

Step 4 Many different types of fans can be attached to a CPU in many different ways. Describe the characteristics of the types of fans shown in Figure 2-2.

_____

_____

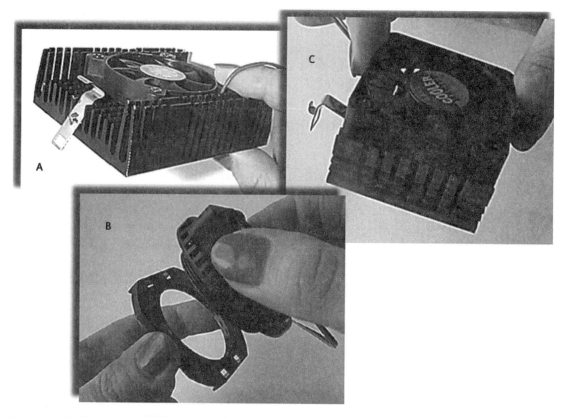

Figure 2-2 Comparing different CPU fans

Step 5   Shut down your PC and unplug the power cable from the wall socket. Place it on your anti-static mat and remove the cover from the case. Locate your CPU and fan assembly. Make note of the type of CPU package and fan assembly installed, but do not remove it at this time. Also note the type of power connector used for the fan—Molex, three-prong motherboard plug, or none. When finished, replace the PC's case cover, plug the system back in and turn it on.

 30 MINUTES

Lab Exercise 2.02: CPU Sockets and Slots

Because you know your CPUs, you have identified Joe's purchase, but you explain to him that until you look at his motherboard, you can't say whether he'll be able to use it. CPU compatibility is determined largely by the motherboard's support capabilities. Some motherboards enable you to upgrade the PC by replacing the existing CPU with a faster model of the same type. In many cases, however, you're forced to replace the entire motherboard if you want to move up to a faster microprocessor.

Learning Objectives

In this lab, you'll identify various CPU sockets.

At the end of this lab, you'll be able to

- Recognize different kinds of CPU sockets and slots

- Know which CPUs need which sockets or slots

Lab Materials and Setup

The materials you need for this lab are

- One desktop computer system

- One anti-static mat

- A notepad

This lab is more informative if you have access to different types of motherboards with different types of CPU sockets.

Getting Down to Business

In the following steps, you'll review your knowledge of CPU socket types.

Step 1 Identify and describe the different socket types in Figure 2-3. Include the socket number/letter and the make and model of CPU that would fit it.

Example: Socket 7, Intel Pentium and AMD K6 CPUs

A. _____

B. _____

C. _____

D. _____

Step 2 Draw a line connecting each CPU to its corresponding socket type:

CPU	Socket Type
Pentium P54C	Socket 370
Pentium Pro	Slot 1
Celeron (II) 600	Socket A
Pentium 4	Socket 478
Athlon 1200	Socket 8
Pentium II	Socket 7

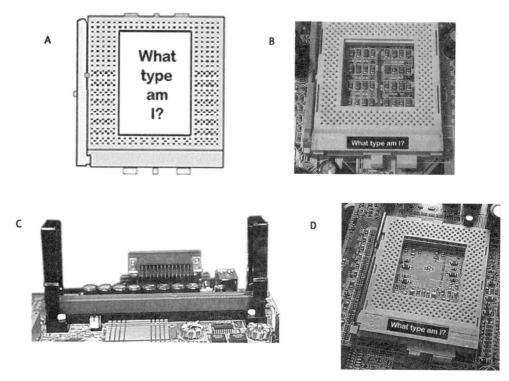

FIGURE 2-3 Identifying sockets

 30 MINUTES

Lab Exercise 2.03: CPU Removal and Installation

Lucky for Joe, his motherboard is compatible with his new CPU. Now he expects you to play your "Computer Expert" role and install the new CPU in his PC. As a PC tech, you must be comfortable with such basic tasks. In this exercise, you'll familiarize yourself with the procedure; first you'll shut down your PC and remove the cover, then you'll remove and reinstall the CPU and fan assembly.

Learning Objectives

In this lab, you'll practice removing and installing a CPU and CPU fan.

At the end of this lab, you'll be able to

- Remove and install a CPU safely and correctly

- Remove and install a CPU fan assembly safely and correctly

Lab Materials and Setup

The materials you need for this lab are

- One fully functioning PC system
- Anti-static mat, or other static-safe material on which to place the CPU following removal
- Anti-static wrist strap
- Thermal paste

Getting Down to Business

Time to get your hands dirty! Removing and installing CPUs is one of the most nerve-wracking tasks that new PC techs undertake, but there's no need to panic. You'll be fine as long as you take the proper precautions to prevent ESD damage, and handle the CPU and fan assembly with care.

> ✖ **Warning**
>
> Be careful not to touch any of the exposed metal contacts on either the CPU or the CPU socket or slot.

Step 1   Shut down and unplug your PC and place it on your anti-static mat. Remove the cover and locate the CPU. If necessary, remove any component cabling that may interfere with removing the CPU and fan assembly. Be sure to label any parts that you have to remove for easier reinstallation later.

Step 2   You may have to remove the fan assembly before you can remove the microprocessor, particularly if your system uses a PGA-type CPU. SEC-type CPUs and fan assemblies are usually removed as a single unit. Screw-down fans are easier to remove than clip fans. Screw-down fans require only that you unscrew the securing hardware. Clip fans, found on pretty much all new CPUs, require you to apply pressure on the clip to release it from the fan mount. Use a small screwdriver to do this, as shown in Figure 2-4. Don't forget to unplug the CPU fan!

FIGURE 2-4 Using a screwdriver to remove a clip-type CPU fan from its mount

✔ **Hint**

You'll discover that releasing a fan clip takes way more force than you would think you should apply to anything so near a delicate CPU chip. Realizing this in advance, you can be sure to brace yourself and position the screwdriver carefully, to minimize the possibility of it slipping off and gouging something.

The CPU and fan assembly will have thermal paste residue on the surfaces that were previously touching. You cannot reuse thermal paste, so you'll need to apply a fresh layer when you reinstall the CPU fan. Using a clean, lint-free cloth, carefully wipe off the thermal paste residue from the CPU and fan assembly, then place the fan assembly on an anti-static surface.

Step 3   Now remove the CPU. Be careful to lift the CPU straight up, *not* at an angle! If you remove a CPU at an angle, you'll bend the tiny pins. Notice the orientation of the CPU's notched edge. Almost all CPUs have them.

There are different methods of removing the chip depending on the type:

Socket-type CPUs   To remove a socket-type CPU, move the Zero Insertion Force (ZIF) lever a little outward to clear the safety notch, and then raise it to a perpendicular position. Next, grasp the chip carefully by its edges and lift it straight up out of the socket. Be careful not to move the chip sideways at all, or you'll bend the pins. Also make sure that the lever stays in an upright position.

SEC-type CPUs   Removing Single Edge Contact Cartridge (SEC) CPU chips that use a slot interface normally does not require removing the fan, which is usually attached to the chip cartridge itself. To remove a slot CPU, first check for and release any retaining clips that may be securing it to the slot, and then grasp the cartridge firmly on both ends and pull straight up from the motherboard.

Step 4   Now that you have the CPU chip out, examine it closely. The manufacturer usually prints the chip's brand and type directly on the chip, providing you with some important facts about the chip's design and performance capabilities. If your chip is an Intel Celeron II 600, for example, you know that its PGA packaging fits in a Socket 370, its bus speed is 66 MHz, and it runs at 600 MHz. Make a note of the relevant specs for your chip.

What is the CPU information printed on the chip package?

_____

✖ **Warning**

Always handle a CPU chip like it's a fragile old photograph: very gently, holding it only by the edges. Make sure you take *complete* ESD precautions because even a tiny amount of static electricity can harm a CPU chip!

Step 5 Reinsert the CPU, and reattach the fan. Be sure to apply a thin film of fresh thermal paste onto the square in the center of the top of the CPU before you place the fan. Don't forget to plug the fan back in.

Step 6 Turn your system back on to make sure you have the CPU seated properly. Always test this before you put the case back on.

Step 7 Put the cover back on the PC case and secure it.

Lab Analysis Test

1. James has an AMD Duron CPU motherboard and has bought a faster Intel Pentium III CPU from an eBay auction. He asked you to install the new CPU. What is your first reaction?

2. Joanna called you and stated that ever since you installed her new CPU the PC gives intermittent problems when it runs. Sometimes it just quits and freezes up. What could possibly be wrong?

3. Teresa has a Socket 7 motherboard with an AMD K6 and would like to put in a faster CPU. Can she install an Intel Celeron 700? Why or why not?

4. Debbie has purchased a new Pentium II slot 1 CPU. She needs a fan. Will a hinge-clip fan work okay? Why or why not?

5. David heard somewhere that the size of the data bus is important to the overall speed of the system. Is this true? Explain.

Key Term Quiz

Use the following vocabulary terms to complete the following sentences. Not all of the terms will be used.

clip connector

CPU

fan assembly

microprocessor

package

slot

socket

1. The Intel Pentium II CPU uses a _____ connection.

2. The AMD K6 uses a _____ connection.

3. CPUs have their own _____ for cooling.

4. Another name for a CPU is _____.

5. One common type of CPU fan connector is the _____.

Chapter 3
RAM

Lab Exercises

One of the easiest and most cost-effective upgrades you can make to a PC is to add more memory. As such, RAM installation is probably the most common type of upgrade you'll perform as a PC tech.

RAM installation tasks include determining how much RAM the PC has installed, how much RAM the PC can support, what type of RAM it uses, and physically installing the RAM on the motherboard. The following labs are designed to give you practice working with RAM by using visual recognition of the different types and packages and by walking you through the steps of installing RAM.

 15 MINUTES

Lab Exercise 3.01: Determining the Amount of RAM in Your PC

So there you are, a week after upgrading Joe's CPU (see Chapter 2), using your lunch hour to frag your fellow PC techs in Half Life, when who should show up again but Joe, this time clutching a stick of RAM he got from a guy on the fourth floor. He wants you to install it in his system. You tell him you have to check on some things first, including how much RAM his system can hold, and how much is already in it, before you can help him. He doesn't know, and you don't recall, how much RAM he has installed already, so that's your first task. Then you must research the RAM capacity of his system.

> ✔ **Hint**
>
> High-end PCs usually come straight from the factory equipped with hefty amounts of RAM. One of the areas where makers of lower-cost PCs cut corners is by skimping on RAM.

Your first task in performing a RAM upgrade is determining how much RAM you need. Start by finding out how much RAM is currently installed on the system, and then consult with the motherboard's documentation to determine how much RAM the system supports.

Learning Objectives

In this lab exercise, you'll use various methods to determine how much memory is currently installed in your system, and how much it is capable of holding.

At the end of this lab, you'll

- Understand where to find RAM measurements

- Be able to determine how much RAM is installed in a system

- Be able to determine how much RAM a particular motherboard supports

Lab Materials and Setup

The materials you need for this lab are

- A working Windows PC

- A notepad

✔ **Hint**

If you're in a computer lab or you have access to multiple PCs, you should practice on as many different PCs as possible.

Getting Down to Business

There are several ways to determine how much RAM is installed on a PC. First, you can check the RAM count during POST. This tells you how much RAM the system BIOS recognizes during its check of the system. Second, you can check the amount of RAM that Windows recognizes from within the OS. And third, you can remove the PC case cover and physically examine the RAM sticks installed on the motherboard.

✔ **Cross-Reference**

To review the ways you can check the amount of RAM installed in a PC, refer to the "Determining Current RAM Capacity" section of Chapter 3 of *Mike Meyers' A+ Guide to PC Hardware*.

Step 1 Turn on your PC, and watch the display as the system goes through the POST routine. Typically, the RAM count runs near the top-left side of the screen. Figure 3-1 shows an example of a typical RAM count.

Most BIOS programs display the RAM count in kilobytes (KB). To convert this figure to megabytes (MB), divide it by 1,024.

Many systems run through the POST routine quickly, so the RAM count may only appear onscreen for a few seconds. Press the PAUSE/BREAK key to pause the boot process so you have time to write down the number accurately. When you want the count to restart, press the ENTER key.

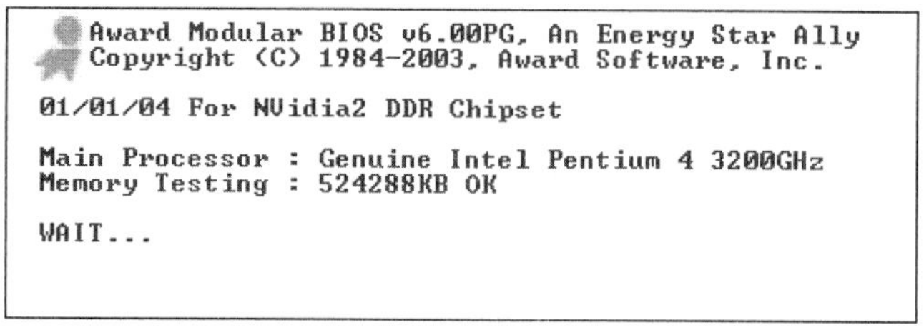

```
Award Modular BIOS v6.00PG, An Energy Star Ally
Copyright (C) 1984-2003, Award Software, Inc.

01/01/04 For NVidia2 DDR Chipset

Main Processor : Genuine Intel Pentium 4 3200GHz
Memory Testing : 524288KB OK

WAIT...
```

FIGURE 3-1 Viewing a typical RAM count during POST

What is the RAM count number displayed on your monitor? _____

✔ **Hint**

If you're starting the PC for the first time of the day, the POST routine may run through the RAM count before the monitor has a chance to warm up. If this happens, just reboot the PC and try again.

Depending on your system's BIOS, you may also see a RAM count in the system configuration summary. This is a screen that lists the PC's CPU type and clock speed, mass storage devices, port addresses, and so on. Typically, you'll also see an entry for the system's base memory (640 KB) and extended memory (the total amount of RAM installed).

Step 2   Use the following methods to determine the amount of RAM on your system from within any version of Windows.

    a)   Alternate-click the My Computer icon and select Properties to see the amount of RAM in your system (see Figure 3-2).

    b)   You'll notice that Windows shows RAM as megabytes instead of kilobytes, but the numbers add up to the same total amount.

Another way to see the amount of memory installed is to follow this procedure:

    a)   Click Start | Programs (or All Programs in Windows XP) | Accessories | System Tools | System Information. In the System Summary, look for a value called Total Physical Memory (see Figure 3-3).

    b)   The amount of RAM will be located in the displayed information.

How much memory is in your system? _____

Does the number agree with step 1 previously? _____

We'll save the last method for determining how much RAM is installed on the system for the next exercise in this lab. For the moment, let's talk about how to determine the maximum amount of RAM your system is capable of supporting.

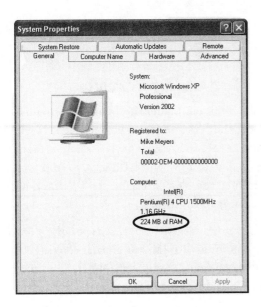

Figure 3-2 Viewing the RAM count in
Windows XP via My Computer

Step 3 Because modern versions of the Windows OS are able to address up to 4 gigabytes (GB) of physical RAM, the amount of RAM you can install on a modern system depends on the limitations of the motherboard hardware.

Neither the CMOS nor the OS can help you determine how much RAM a PC is *capable* of handling. The best source for this information is the system's motherboard documentation, if you have it, or the PC maker's or motherboard manufacturer's web site.

Examine the documentation that came with your PC, or visit the manufacturer's web site to determine how much RAM you can install on the system. What is the maximum amount of RAM that your system can support? _____

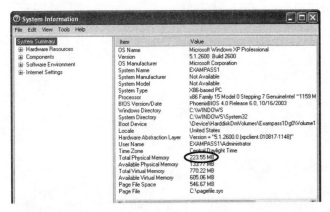

Figure 3-3 Viewing the System Information showing
Total Physical Memory

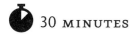 30 MINUTES

Lab Exercise 3.02: Identifying Types of RAM

Once you determine how much RAM Joe has installed, and how much his motherboard can handle, you conclude that there's room for more. But, you explain to Joe, that doesn't mean you can add this RAM stick, because not all RAM is the same. Having looked at the specs for his system, you know it takes 168-pin DIMMs. Joe thinks the stick he got is the right size to fit, but you know it's DDR RAM, so it won't. This is why they pay you the big bucks. And why you get to take the RAM stick Joe can't use and add it to your own machine! (Juuust kidding! Of course you'd return it to inventory.)

RAM comes in several standardized form factors, each compatible with specific types of systems. Modern desktop systems use full-sized Dual Inline Memory Modules (DIMMs) or similar-looking RIMMs. Older desktop models may still support banks of Single Inline Memory Modules (SIMMs). Laptop computers use scaled-down DIMM versions called Small Outline DIMMs, or SO-DIMMs.

✔ **Cross-Reference**

For details on the various types of RAM found in modern systems, refer to the "RAM Sticks Part II" and "Improvements in DRAM Technology" sections of Chapter 3 of *Mike Meyers' A+ Guide to PC Hardware.*

Steps for identifying the different types of RAM are listed below.

Learning Objectives

In this lab, you'll examine and compare different RAM packages.

At the end of this lab, you'll be able to

- Recognize and differentiate between different kinds of RAM packages

Lab Materials and Setup

The materials you need for this lab are

- A working computer with RAM installed

- Demonstration units of various RAM packages (optional)

FIGURE 3-4 A 72-pin SIMM

✔ **Hint**

It is helpful to examine the RAM configurations in multiple PCs, if you have them available. Having a laptop with removable RAM is a plus.

Getting Down to Business

Let's do a quick review of the types of RAM packages that you'll see on modern PCs. Then you'll check your PC or motherboard documentation to determine the type of RAM it uses. Finally, you'll take the cover off of your PC to determine what type of RAM is installed.

Step 1   Your motherboard most likely has one of the following three types of RAM packages:

72-pin SIMMs   Single Inline Memory Modules (SIMMs) are about four inches long and have 72 physical pins (edge connectors) on each side, but only one side is actually used for operation. The board has a notch in the bottom center that is offset slightly (see Figure 3-4). You'll only find SIMM RAM on very old PCs.

168-pin DIMMs   These are about five inches long and have 84 physical pins (edge connectors) on each side, and all 168 connectors are used. The board has two notches on the bottom: one near the center, and the other near an end (see Figure 3-5).

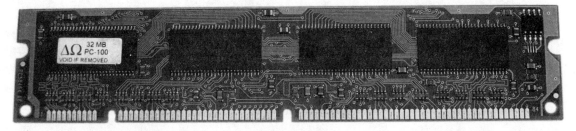

FIGURE 3-5 A 168-pin DIMM

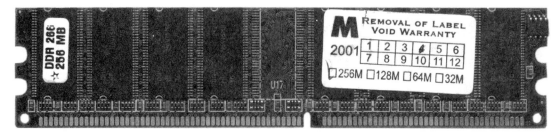

FIGURE 3-6 A 184-pin DDR DIMM

184-pin DDR DIMMs   DDR RAM sticks are about five inches long and look just like 168-pin DIMMs but have only one notch and more connectors. These are known as Double Date Rate (DDR) memory. The notches are different from 168-pin DIMMs, so they cannot be interchanged with each other (see Figure 3-6).

184-pin RIMMs   *Rambus Dynamic RAM* (RDRAM) is the type of RAM you'll find on the latest high-end systems intended for power-hungry applications like video editing and 3-D games. You call a stick of RDRAM a RIMM. RIMM is actually trademarked as a word; it's not an acronym like DIMM, despite what many people assume (see Figure 3-7).

Step 2   In your PC or motherboard documentation, locate the section listing the type of RAM your system uses. What speed of RAM does your system need? _____

Step 3   Shut down and unplug your PC, then remove the case cover and locate the RAM. Do not remove the RAM at this point, but make note of

How many RAM slots does your motherboard have? _____

How many RAM slots are filled with RAM sticks? _____

Can you tell at a glance whether your system has SIMMs, DIMMs, DDR DIMMs, or RIMMs? _____

FIGURE 3-7 A 184-pin RIMM

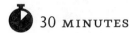 30 MINUTES

Lab Exercise 3.03: Removing and Installing RAM

Taking pity on Joe, you found a stick of RAM for him that works with his system, and now you have to install it. Meanwhile, you can reinventory that stick of DDR RAM into your computer!

Although RAM installation is one of the simpler PC hardware upgrades, it's still important that you follow the correct steps and take all appropriate safety precautions.

Learning Objectives

In this lab, you'll practice removing and installing RAM.

At the end of this lab, you'll be able to

- Remove RAM safely and correctly

- Install RAM safely and correctly

Lab Materials and Setup

The materials you need for this lab are

- A working PC

- Anti-static mat or other static-safe material on which to place the RAM

- Anti-static wrist strap

- A notepad

✔ Hint

If you're in a computer lab or you have access to multiple PCs, you should practice on a variety of systems.

Getting Down to Business

Removal and installation procedures vary depending on the type of RAM your system uses. DIMMs and RIMMs snap into the RAM slots vertically, while SIMMs are installed at an angle and pivoted into their final locked position. The following steps describe the removal and installation procedures for each type of RAM.

✖ Warning

Regardless of the type of RAM on your system, be certain to take measures to prevent ESD damage. Shut down and unplug your PC and place it on your anti-static mat. Strap on your anti-static bracelet and ground yourself. If necessary, remove any cables or components that block access to your system RAM before you begin.

✔ Cross-Reference

For further review of the RAM installation process, refer to the "Installing SIMMs and Installing DIMMs and RIMMs" sections of Chapter 3 of *Mike Meyers' A+ Guide to PC Hardware.*

Follow these steps to remove DIMM or RIMM RAM from your PC:

Step 1   Locate the retention clips on either end of the DIMM stick.

Step 2   Press outward on the clips to disengage them from the retention slots on the sides of the RAM sticks (see Figure 3-8).

Step 3   Press down on the clips firmly and evenly. The retention clips act as levers to lift the DIMM sticks up and slightly out of the RAM slots.

Step 4   Remove the DIMM sticks and place them on your anti-static mat, or some other static-safe material.

FIGURE 3-8 Removing a 168-pin DIMM

Step 5   Make note of the following:

How many pins does your RAM have? _____

Where are the guide notches located? _____

What information is on the RAM's label? _____

Follow these steps to remove SIMM RAM from your PC:

Step 1   Locate the retention clips on either end of the SIMM sticks. Remember that SIMMs require two RAM sticks to make a complete memory bank.

Step 2   Press outward on the clips to disengage them from the retention slots on the sides of the RAM sticks. Some motherboards don't leave you with much room to operate, so you may need a small screwdriver or needle nose pliers to undo the retention clips. Be *very* careful not to touch any of the circuitry with metal tools!

Step 3   Once the SIMMs are loose, pivot them down to a 45-degree angle and slide them out (see Figure 3-9).

Step 4   Place the SIMMs on your anti-static mat, or some other static-safe material.

Step 5   Make note of the following:

How many pins does your RAM have? _____

Where is the guide notch located? _____

What information is on the RAM's label? _____

Figure 3-9 Removing a 72-pin SIMM

Step 6   While you've got your system RAM out, this is a good time to check the condition of the metal contacts on both the RAM sticks and the motherboard RAM sockets.

Are they dirt- and corrosion-free? _____

After you've examined your system RAM and inspected the motherboard RAM sockets, reinstall the RAM as described below.

To install DIMM or RIMM RAM:

Step 1   Orient the DIMM or RIMM RAM sticks so that the guide notches on the RAM match up to the guide ridges on the RAM sockets.

Step 2   Press the RAM sticks firmly and evenly down into the sockets until the retention clips engage the retention notches on the ends of the RAM sticks.

Step 3   Snap the retention clips firmly into place.

Step 4   If using RIMM RAM, don't forget to install the *Continuity RIMM* (CRIMM) sticks into any empty RAM slots.

To install SIMM RAM:

Step 1   Orient the SIMM RAM stick so that the guide notch on the end matches the guide ridge on the socket.

Step 2   Slide the RAM stick into the socket at a 45-degree angle until it seats firmly.

Step 3   Pivot the RAM upward until it snaps into place, making sure that both retention clips are secured.

To finish a RAM installation:

Step 1   Once your system RAM is in place, reattach any cables that you may have had to move, and plug the system power cable in. Do not reinstall the PC case cover until after you've confirmed that RAM installation was successful.

Step 2   Boot the system up and watch the RAM count to confirm that you correctly installed the RAM sticks.

✔ Hint

If your system has any problems when you reboot, remember that you must turn off the power and unplug the computer before reseating the RAM.

Lab Analysis Test

1. Kal wants to upgrade his memory and calls you for help. He can't find the documentation for his motherboard, but describes it for you. He says it has three RAM slots. Only one is filled. What kind of RAM does he have?

   _____

   _____

2. Teresa's Windows 2000 Professional system has 128 MB of RAM. She adds 256 MB of RAM, but the RAM count still only shows 128 MB. What could be causing this?

   _____

   _____

3. John's system has 256 MB of PC100 RAM. He recently installed an additional 512 MB of RAM that a coworker gave him. He tells you that his system now boots up correctly and shows the correct amount of RAM, but that it freezes after several minutes. He notes that if he removes the new RAM, the system runs fine. What could be a possible reason for this?

   _____

   _____

4. Scott is upgrading his laptop computer. What kind of RAM should he buy?

   _____

   _____

5. Joe reads that RDRAM is faster than the SDRAM that he has installed on his system and wants to know if he can simply swap out his current RAM for RDRAM RIMMs. What do you tell him?

   _____

   _____

Key Term Quiz

Use the following vocabulary terms to complete the following sentences. Not all of the terms will be used.

168-pin DIMM

72-pin SIMM

CRIMM

DIMM

DDR RAM

EDO

megabytes (MB)

RIMM

SDRAM

SO-DIMM

1. Today's PCs have RAM measured in _____ of memory.

2. A RAM module used in a laptop is called a(n) _____.

3. A _____ is inserted at a 45-degree angle and then snapped up into place.

4. A stick of _____ looks a lot like a 168-pin DIMM, but it has 184 pins.

5. On systems that use RIMMs, empty RAM sockets must be filled by _____.

Chapter 4
BIOS and CMOS

Lab Exercises

Basic input/output services (BIOS) provide the primary interface between the operating system's device drivers and most of the hardware of your system. Although modern BIOS is automated and tolerant of misconfiguration, a good PC technician must be comfortable with those occasional situations where BIOS may need some maintenance or repair.

BIOS is necessary in the PC to give it the instructions for how each different basic component is to communicate with the system. At the beginning of the PC revolution, many different manufacturers developed BIOS for PCs, but over the years the BIOS business has consolidated to only three brands—AMI, Award Software, and Phoenix Technologies. Each of these manufacturers provides a utility called the *CMOS setup program* (CMOS stands for *complementary metal-oxide semiconductor*) that enables you to reconfigure BIOS settings for things such as boot device order, IRQ reservations, amount of memory, hard disk drive configuration, and so on. As a PC tech, you'll find yourself doing this more often than you might think!

As an example, let's say that your company is planning a mass upgrade from your current OS—Windows 98—to Windows XP Professional. You've tested the upgrade process on a few lab machines, and found that systems with out-of-date BIOS have had problems upgrading successfully. In preparation for Windows XP installation, besides upgrading any older BIOS versions you find, you'll disable any BIOS-level antivirus checking functions.

The lab exercises in this chapter will teach you to identify, access, and configure system BIOS.

 10 MINUTES

Lab Exercise 4.01: Identifying BIOS ROM

Having received your orders to do the big OS upgrade, your first task is to check the BIOS types and versions on all the machines in your office, and then visit the BIOS maker's web site to determine if there are more recent versions available.

The system BIOS is stored on non-volatile memory called BIOS ROM. BIOS makers label their BIOS ROM chips prominently on the motherboard. In this exercise, you'll look at two different ways to identify your BIOS ROM chip.

✔ **Cross-Reference**

For details on the various possible physical manifestations of BIOS on modern systems, refer to the "Modern CMOS" section of Chapter 4 of *Mike Meyers' A+ Guide to PC Hardware*.

Learning Objectives

In this lab, you'll learn two ways to identify your BIOS.

At the end of this lab, you'll be able to

- Locate the BIOS ROM chip on the motherboard

- Identify the BIOS manufacturer

- Determine the BIOS creation date and version

Lab Materials and Setup

The materials you need for this lab are

- A working PC

- Anti-static mat

- A notepad

Getting Down to Business

The first thing you'll do is remove your PC case cover and locate the BIOS ROM chip. Next, you'll make note of the BIOS information displayed during system startup.

✖ Warning

Any time you take the cover off of your PC, remember to follow all proper safety and ESD precautions.

Step 1 Remove the case from the PC and locate the system BIOS ROM chip. Look for a chip with a shiny printed label on it. Compare your system BIOS ROM chip to the one in Figure 4-1.

Read the manufacturer's label if you can, and answer the following questions:

Who made the BIOS? _____

What year was the BIOS written? _____

Are there any other numbers on the label? Record them. _____

Does it look like you could easily remove the system BIOS chip, or does it look soldered to the motherboard? _____

Step 2 Replace the PC case cover and start the system. Be sure the monitor is turned on. When the first data appears on the screen, press the PAUSE/BREAK key on the keyboard. This suspends further operation until you press ENTER.

Figure 4-2 shows an example of what you may see. At the top of the screen is the BIOS manufacturer's name and version number. At the bottom of the screen is the date of manufacture and the product identification number.

FIGURE 4-1 A typical system BIOS ROM chip

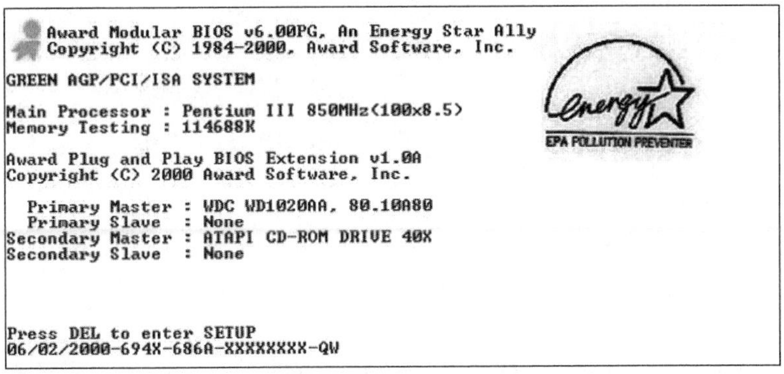

```
   Award Modular BIOS v6.00PG, An Energy Star Ally
   Copyright (C) 1984-2000, Award Software, Inc.

GREEN AGP/PCI/ISA SYSTEM

Main Processor : Pentium III 850MHz(100x8.5)
Memory Testing : 114688K

Award Plug and Play BIOS Extension v1.0A
Copyright (C) 2000 Award Software, Inc.

  Primary Master  : WDC WD1020AA, 80.10A80
  Primary Slave   : None
Secondary Master  : ATAPI CD-ROM DRIVE 40X
Secondary Slave   : None



Press DEL to enter SETUP
06/02/2000-694X-686A-XXXXXXXX-QW
```

FIGURE 4-2 A typical boot screen

Make note of the following information:

Who made the BIOS? _____

What version is the BIOS? _____

What year was the BIOS written? _____

✔ **Hint**

Not all BIOS display the same type of information. Some BIOS makers modify the BIOS to show nothing more their logos during the boot process.

Step 3   Press ENTER on the keyboard to continue booting. Once the system is up and running, go online and find out if there is a more recent version of your BIOS available. Your first stop should be your PC maker's web site. If they do not have this information available, try your motherboard manufacturer or the BIOS maker.

✖ **Warning**

Do NOT "flash" your system BIOS at this time!

 15 MINUTES

Lab Exercise 4.02: Accessing BIOS via the CMOS Setup Program

Once you've assessed and, where necessary, upgraded the BIOS on each machine, before you proceed with the Windows XP installation, you should check to be sure the BIOS is properly configured, using the special program for this purpose.

You don't access the hundreds of individual programs contained in the system BIOS directly, or from anywhere within the Windows OS. Instead, you use a utility that interfaces with the BIOS programs to enable you to reconfigure settings. This utility is the CMOS setup program.

Learning Objectives

In this lab, you'll go into CMOS and explore your BIOS configuration settings.

At the end of this lab, you'll be able to

- Enter the CMOS setup program

- Navigate the display screens of the setup utility

Lab Materials and Setup

The materials you need for this lab are

- A working PC whose BIOS settings you can change

Getting Down to Business

In the following steps, you'll reboot your PC and access the CMOS setup program. BIOS makers each have their own special way to do this, so how you go about it depends on which BIOS your system has installed. Common methods include

- Press DELETE during the boot process.

- Press F2 during the boot process.

- Press F10 during the boot process.

- Press CTRL-ALT-INSERT during the boot process.

- Press CTRL-A during the boot process.

- Press CTRL-F1 during the boot process.

There are four ways for you to determine which method works for your BIOS:

- Check your motherboard or PC documentation.

- Visit your motherboard- or PC-maker's web site.

- Watch the screen display after booting your PC. Most direct you to press a specific key needed to enter CMOS.

- Trial and error. Boot your system and go down the list trying each key or key combination listed previously. You won't hurt anything if you get it wrong, but if you hold the wrong key down for too long you may get a keyboard error message. If this happens, just reboot and try again.

Step 1   Determine which method you need to use to enter the CMOS setup program. Then reboot your system and use that method to enter CMOS.

Step 2   Once you've entered the CMOS setup program, look at the screen and compare it to Figures 4-3 and 4-4. The Phoenix BIOS shown in Figure 4-3 opens immediately into the Main screen, while the Award BIOS in Figure 4-4 presents an initial menu. Although the screens for different CMOS setup programs may look different, they all contain basically the same functions.

✖ **Warning**

Do not make any changes in BIOS settings during this lab exercise. You'll make changes in the next lab.

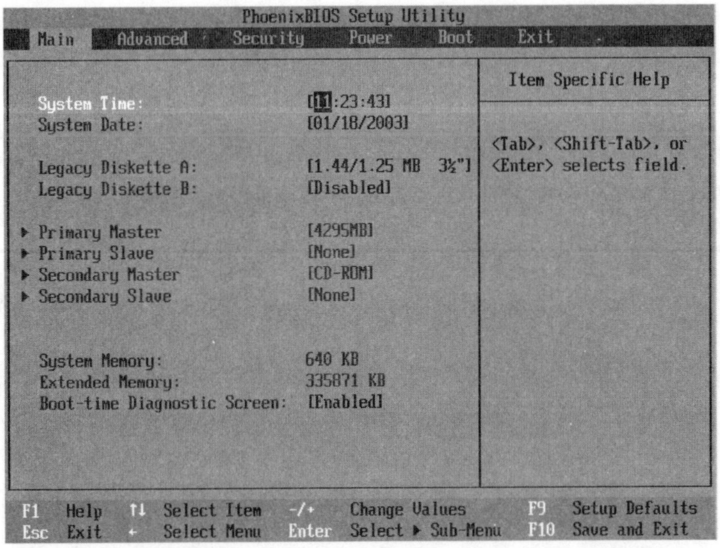

FIGURE 4-3 Phoenix CMOS Main screen

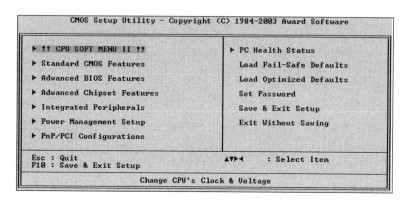

FIGURE 4-4 Award BIOS opening screen

The CMOS setup program controls the "changeable" BIOS settings. Many settings depend on what you add to the system. The following are some sample entries on your system you can change or update (there are more depending on your BIOS):

- Date

- Time

- Hard drive configuration

- Boot sequence

- RAM

- IRQ reservations

- Serial and parallel port assignments

- Enable/disable onboard controllers

Step 3   Explore each screen and make notes about what each one does. Navigation, like the method to enter the CMOS setup program, varies from maker to maker. Most are navigable by keyboard only, but some (AMI, for instance) support a mouse. Look at the bottom of the CMOS setup program screen to see how to navigate in your particular CMOS utility.

 Hint

Usually the arrow keys and the PAGE UP and PAGE DOWN keys will select and change settings.

Step 4   Record some of the more common settings here for a review reference. View every screen of your CMOS setup utility to locate these settings and record them:

Primary Master (Type) _____

Drive A _____

Video _____

Halt On _____

Boot Sequence _____

Resources Controlled By _____

FDC Controller _____

Serial Port 1 _____

Parallel Port Mode _____

Once you're done exploring, press ESC a couple of times until you get the message "Quit Without Saving (Y/N)?" Press Y, and then press ENTER. The system will boot into your operating system.

 30 MINUTES

Lab Exercise 4.03: Configuring BIOS Settings

If you find any issues when you examine the BIOS settings using the CMOS setup program, you'll need to reconfigure the settings. Remember also that you're preparing the PC for an upgrade to Windows XP Professional. BIOS-level virus checking is known to cause problems with the Windows 2000/XP installation process, and so Microsoft advises that you disable it.

Many BIOS functions are unchangeable, and therefore inaccessible via the CMOS setup program. These include things like keyboard and floppy drive recognition. Other things are under your control. These include the previously mentioned things like boot sequence order and the date/time, but also some potentially hazardous settings such as BIOS shadowing and memory timing.

✔ **Hint**

If you're not absolutely certain what a particular setting does, the best course of action is to leave it alone! If you have any doubts, you can always exit the CMOS setup program without saving.

Learning Objectives

In this exercise, you'll access the CMOS setup utility and navigate through to find the various BIOS settings you would commonly need to modify, and practice disabling BIOS-level virus checking.

At the end of this lab, you'll be able to

- Modify the settings in BIOS

Lab Materials and Setup

The materials you need for this lab are

- A working PC whose BIOS settings you can change

- If possible, a BIOS that includes virus checking

Getting Down to Business

In the steps listed below, you'll learn to navigate to the CMOS setup program configuration screen that has the virus checking option. This example uses the Award BIOS CMOS setup program. Your CMOS setup program may vary, but all BIOS makers and versions should offer the same option.

✔ **Cross-Reference**

> For more details about the features of CMOS setup programs, refer to the section called "A Quick Tour Through a Typical CMOS Setup" in Chapter 4 of *Mike Meyers' A+ Guide to PC Hardware*.

Step 1   Enter your CMOS setup program using the steps you learned in Lab Exercise 4.02.

Step 2   Check your notes and navigate to the configuration screen that has the BIOS-level virus checking options. It's not always obvious where to find this option. For example, the Award BIOS CMOS setup program screen shown in Figure 4-4 doesn't give any hints about where to find the correct screen. As Figure 4-5 shows, virus checking can be disabled in this BIOS from the Advanced BIOS Features screen. Don't hesitate to explore.

Step 3   Follow the screen prompts to navigate to the correct configuration screen and find the virus checking setting option. Highlight the option (either using the arrow keys or mouse), and change it from Enabled to Disabled. Once again, your CMOS setup programs' wording or appearance may be different, but the option to turn BIOS-level virus checking should be common to all modern BIOS.

Step 4   Save and exit the CMOS setup program. After you exit, the system will reboot automatically. You have just made a change to BIOS.

The process you just followed is the same process you'll use for any changes you make to BIOS. Be sure to save the settings before exiting the setup utility.

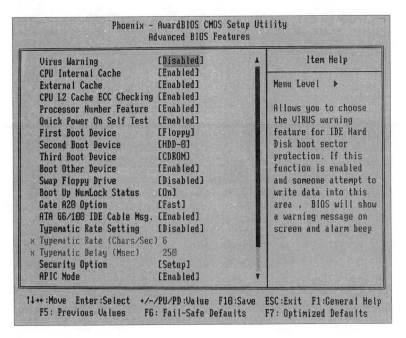

```
             Phoenix - AwardBIOS CMOS Setup Utility
                     Advanced BIOS Features

    Virus Warning             [Disabled]   ▲  │      Item Help
    CPU Internal Cache        [Enabled]       │
    External Cache            [Enabled]       │  Menu Level   ▶
    CPU L2 Cache ECC Checking [Enabled]       │
    Processor Number Feature  [Enabled]       │  Allows you to choose
    Quick Power On Self Test  [Enabled]       │  the VIRUS warning
    First Boot Device         [Floppy]        │  feature for IDE Hard
    Second Boot Device        [HDD-0]         │  Disk boot sector
    Third Boot Device         [CDROM]         │  protection. If this
    Boot Other Device         [Enabled]       │  function is enabled
    Swap Floppy Drive         [Disabled]      │  and someone attempt to
    Boot Up NumLock Status    [On]            │  write data into this
    Gate A20 Option           [Fast]          │  area , BIOS will show
    ATA 66/100 IDE Cable Msg. [Enabled]       │  a warning message on
    Typematic Rate Setting    [Disabled]      │  screen and alarm beep
  x Typematic Rate (Chars/Sec) 6              │
  x Typematic Delay (Msec)    250             │
    Security Option           [Setup]         │
    APIC Mode                 [Enabled]    ▼  │

  ↑↓→←:Move  Enter:Select  +/-/PU/PD:Value  F10:Save  ESC:Exit  F1:General Help
     F5: Previous Values     F6: Fail-Safe Defaults    F7: Optimized Defaults
```

FIGURE 4-5 Disabling BIOS-level virus checking

Lab Analysis Test

1. Kathy has noticed recently that when she boots the system it displays a CMOS Mismatch message. What could be the problem?

_____

_____

2. In what situations do you usually need to configure the BIOS?

_____

_____

3. What are some of the BIOS settings you can change using CMOS setup?

_____

_____

4. Name two ways to save the BIOS settings after you've made changes in the CMOS setup program.

_____

_____

5. What key or keys do you press to enter the CMOS setup program?

_____

_____

Key Term Quiz

Use the following vocabulary terms to complete the following sentences. Not all of the terms will be used.

AMI

Award Software

BIOS (basic input/output services)

BIOS ROM

CMOS (complementary metal-oxide semiconductor)

CMOS setup program

DELETE key

PAUSE/BREAK key

Phoenix Technologies

1. The system BIOS is stored on non-volatile memory called _____.

2. Technicians configure the BIOS using the _____.

3. Press the _____ to suspend operation of the POST.

4. _____ provide the primary interface between the operating system's device drivers and most of the system's hardware.

5. A common way to enter CMOS setup is to press the _____ during startup.

Chapter 5

Expansion Bus

Lab Exercises

One of the many things that makes PCs so useful is their amazing versatility. Modern PCs support a wide array of peripheral devices and attachments that expand their capabilities and boost performance. Peripherals attach to the PC via the *expansion bus*.

The expansion bus is the pathway that enables you to plug new devices and device controllers into the motherboard. This pathway can be split up into two groups: the internal expansion bus and the external expansion bus.

The internal expansion bus includes the Peripheral Component Interconnect (PCI) bus, Accelerated Graphics Port (AGP) bus, and on older systems, the Industry Standard Architecture (ISA) bus. Other, specialized internal buses, such as Audio/Modem Riser (AMR) and Communication Network Riser (CNR), also pop up on some systems. The external expansion bus includes the Universal Serial Bus (USB) and the IEEE 1394 (FireWire) bus.

In these lab exercises, you'll learn how to determine which expansion slots are available in a system and how to install and remove expansion cards properly. This will help you gain confidence in handling expansion card issues in the real world.

For the purposes of this chapter, suppose that you're consulting for a small computer graphics firm. Currently, the company has 20 workstation computers of various makes and models, running Windows NT, Windows 2000 Professional, and Windows XP Professional. None of the computers are networked, and each has its own copy of a computer-aided design (CAD) application installed on it. The company wants to upgrade to a newer version of the CAD program, which runs on a high-end application server that each client workstation will need to access via the network.

Additionally, the client company is in the early stages of expanding its services to include editing digital video, so they want to test a video editing application and some related hardware on a few of their workstations.

To accommodate the CAD program upgrade, each client workstation has to have at least a 600 MHz CPU, 256 MB of RAM, a version of Windows based on the NT kernel, an AGP video card with 32 MB of VRAM, and a 10/100BaseT Network Interface Card (NIC). The digital video equipment requires an IEEE 1394 (FireWire) connection on the PC.

You've determined that each computer meets the CPU and RAM requirements to run the CAD application and the video editing program. You have also determined that the machines running Windows NT need to be upgraded to Windows 2000 or XP to accommodate the FireWire requirement. Your task now is to inventory the client's hardware to determine which PCs meet the AGP video card, NIC, and FireWire hardware requirements, and what upgrades need to be made to those system that don't meet the requirements.

 30 MINUTES

Lab Exercise 5.01: Identifying Internal Expansion Slots and External Expansion Connectors

Unless you've got X-ray vision, the best way to examine the expansion slots is to remove the PC case cover. In this exercise, you'll identify the type of expansion slots on your system to see whether the video card is an AGP or PCI model. You'll also check to see how many other expansion slots are available for adding a NIC, and whether or not the system has built-in FireWire support.

✖ Warning

Remember to use proper safety and electrostatic discharge (ESD) procedures when working inside the PC case.

Learning Objectives

In this exercise, you'll properly identify expansion slots and know the basic features of each.

At the end of this lab, you'll be able to

- Identify legacy ISA expansion bus slots and component cards

- Identify PCI expansion bus slots and component cards

- Identify the AGP expansion bus slot and video card

- Identify USB and FireWire external expansion bus connectors and devices

Lab Materials and Setup

One working PC is adequate for this exercise, but it's more beneficial to be able to see motherboards inside different systems.

The materials you need for this lab are

- A working PC (or more than one if possible)

- Anti-static mat

- Notepad

- Sample motherboards (optional)

Getting Down to Business

Shut down your PC and unplug it from the wall. Place it on your anti-static mat, remove the PC case cover, and take a good look inside. Your aim is to determine what type of expansion slots exist on the motherboard, and what peripheral card components are currently installed. You'll also determine which external expansion connectors are supported.

Step 1   Let's start with the old before we move on to the new. Locate any ISA expansion slots on your motherboard. There are still plenty of legacy systems around that have the 16-bit ISA expansion slots. Here are the physical characteristics of ISA expansion slots:

- About five inches long

- Usually black in color

- Offset from the edge of the motherboard by about 1/2 inch

- Large metal contacts easily visible inside the slot

- Divided by a small gap into two parts: the 8-bit portion (about three inches long) and the 16-bit portion (one and a half inches long)

Figure 5-1 shows ISA slots alongside other types of slots on a motherboard.

FIGURE 5-1 A group of three ISA slots, at lower right

Record the following information, as applicable, in your notebook:

How many ISA slots are on your motherboard? _____

What ISA devices are installed on your system? _____

How many ISA slots are empty? _____

Step 2 The next type of expansion slot you'll explore is the 32-bit PCI bus. This is the most common type of expansion slot on modern PCs. Here are the physical characteristics of PCI expansion slots:

- About three inches long
- Usually white in color
- Offset from the edge of the motherboard by about one inch

Figure 5-2 shows PCI slots on a modern motherboard.

Record the following information in your notebook:

How many PCI slots are on your motherboard? _____

What PCI devices are installed on your system? _____

How many PCI slots are empty? _____

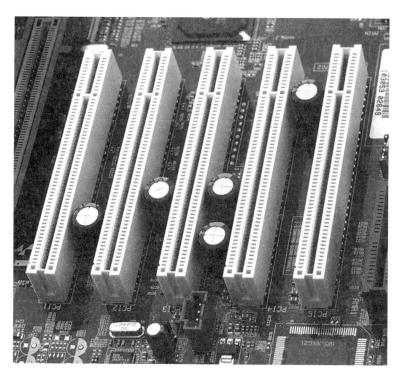

Figure 5-2 A group of PCI slots

Step 3   Now locate the 32-bit AGP slot. As the name suggests, the AGP slot is used for one component only—the video adapter. Here are the physical characteristics of the AGP slot:

- One slot per motherboard

- A little less than three inches long

- Usually brown in color

- Offset from the edge of the motherboard by about two inches

Figure 5-3 shows an AGP slot in its natural habitat.

Record the following information in your notebook:

Is there an AGP video card slot on your motherboard? _____

What can you tell about the type and brand of video card without removing it?

_____

✔ **Cross-Reference**

For more detail about the PCI and AGP buses, refer to the "PCI" section of Chapter 5 of *Mike Meyers' A+ Guide to PC Hardware*.

FIGURE 5-3 An AGP slot

Step 4   Now that you've identified the internal ISA, PCI, and AGP slots on your motherboard, let's look for any external USB or FireWire expansion connectors. USB is practically universal on modern PCs, so chances are good that your system has at least two USB connector sockets (see Figure 5-4). Typically, you'll find the USB connectors near the PS/2 keyboard and mouse connectors on the back of the PC case. Many PCs have additional USB connectors conveniently located on the front or side of the case. If your PC is older, USB connectors may be provided by an add-in USB controller card located in one of your PCI slots.

FireWire support is not quite as universal as USB. Many modern systems do come with FireWire built in, however, and it can also be added via a PCI controller card.

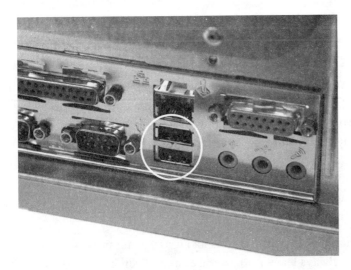

FIGURE 5-4 USB ports

Here are the physical characteristics of USB ports:

- Female-oriented (the USB cable plugs are male)

- Rectangular in shape, with a small plastic "key" to prevent you from inserting the USB cable incorrectly

- About $\frac{1}{2}$ inch wide by $\frac{1}{4}$ inch tall

Record the following information in your notebook:

How many USB ports are on your system? _____

What USB devices are connected to your system? _____

Here are the physical characteristics of FireWire ports:

- Female-oriented (the FireWire cable plugs are male)

- Also rectangular in shape, but rounded at one end to prevent you from inserting the FireWire cable incorrectly

- About $\frac{1}{2}$ inch wide by $\frac{1}{4}$ inch tall

Record the following information in your notebook:

How many FireWire ports are on your system? _____

What FireWire devices are connected to your system? _____

After you've completed your inventory of installed expansion bus devices, put the case cover back on your PC, plug it back in, and restart the system.

 30 MINUTES

Lab Exercise 5.02: Understanding Device Resources

The typical modern PC has many component devices installed: video cards, sound cards, modems, NICs, controller cards (such as SCSI controllers, SATA controllers, and so on), not to mention the built-in devices such as IDE and floppy disk drive controllers. As amazing as it seems, a PC's CPU only talks to one device at a time. This means that at any given time, one device has exclusive access to the CPU. Of course, this happens so quickly that it seems like the CPU is addressing multiple components all at once. The PC keeps track of which device is which is through *system resources*, the collective term for device settings such as input/output (I/O) addresses, interrupt requests (IRQs), Direct Memory Access (DMA) channels, and memory address settings.

On modern PCs, Plug and Play (PnP) handles all of the details about assigning system resources to devices, but this doesn't mean that you can always leave it up to the system! Even as sophisticated as

PnP is, things don't always work as they're supposed to—especially if you're mixing old, non-PnP devices with newer PnP devices. Therefore, it's important for techs to know how to identify a device's system resources and, when necessary, manually configure them.

In the old days, configuring device resources meant setting jumpers and DIP switches on the device and running a setup program supplied by the device maker. If you're using very old, non-PnP devices, this is still the case, but on modern PnP devices, all resource configuration is handled from within the Windows OS. Let's look now at how to determine and configure your component devices' system resource settings.

✔ **Cross-Reference**

If you need a refresher on system resources, refer to the "System Resources" section of Chapter 5 of *Mike Meyers' A+ Guide to PC Hardware*.

Learning Objectives

In this lab, you'll reinforce your knowledge of system resources.

At the end of this lab, you'll be able to

- Understand the basic I/O address and IRQ settings you need for the A+ Certification exam
- Use the Device Manager to find out what I/O addresses are allocated
- Know the rules of assigning IRQs and the default assignments

Lab Materials and Setup

The materials you need for this lab are

- A working computer running Windows

✔ **Hint**

As usual, if you have access to more than one system, take advantage of it.

Getting Down to Business

In this exercise, you'll use the Windows Device Manager to view the system resource settings on your PC.

Step 1 Open the Windows Control Panel and double-click the icon for the System applet. Note that you can also access this applet by pressing the Windows key and the PAUSE/BREAK key at the same time.

FIGURE 5-5 Device Manager
in Windows XP

On Windows 9x systems, you can go directly to Device Manager by selecting the Device Manager tab. On Windows 2000/XP systems, you must first select the Hardware tab, and then click the Device Manager button to bring up the Device Manager in a separate window (see Figure 5-5).

Step 2   Device Manager shows you at a glance all of your system's IRQ, I/O, DMA, and memory address settings for each device. Naturally, the way you do this differs between Windows 9x systems and Windows 2000/XP systems. On a Windows 9x PC, highlight the Computer icon in Device Manager and click the Properties button. This brings up a dialog box where you can select a set of resources to view. In Windows 2000/XP, select View from the menu bar and then click Resource by type, then expand the node for the resource type that you want to investigate (see Figure 5-6).

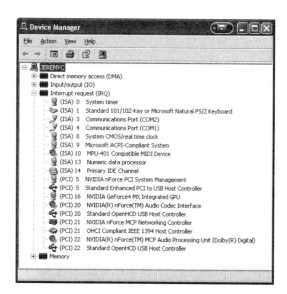

FIGURE 5-6 Viewing system resources

Step 3 Select the option to view the Input/Output (I/O) settings on your system. Scroll down the list to review and locate the address to answer these questions:

What is the address for the keyboard? _____

What is the address for the printer port (LPT1)? _____

What is the address for the system speaker? _____

What is the address for the communications port (COM1)? _____

What is the address for the system timer? _____

Step 4 Repeat steps 1–3, this time looking at the IRQ settings.

Does your system use IRQ 6? _____

What device uses IRQ 6? _____

Step 5 List the three basic rules of I/O addresses.

Rule #1 _____

Rule #2 _____

Rule #3 _____

Step 6 Compare the IRQ settings in the following table to your system, and then answer the questions on the following page:

IRQ	Default Function
IRQ 0	System timer
IRQ 1	Keyboard
IRQ 2/9	Open for use
IRQ 3	Default COM2, COM4
IRQ 4	Default COM1, COM3
IRQ 5	Open for use (or LPT2)
IRQ 6	Floppy drive
IRQ 7	LPT1
IRQ 8	Real-time clock
IRQ 10	Open for use
IRQ 11	Open for use
IRQ 12	Open for use
IRQ 13	Math coprocessor
IRQ 14	Primary hard drive controller
IRQ 15	Secondary hard drive controller

Which IRQs are by default open for use? _____

Which IRQ is by default assigned to LPT1? _____

Which IRQ is by default assigned to the floppy drive? _____

Which IRQ is by default assigned to the primary hard drive controller? _____

Which IRQs are by default assigned to

COM1? _____

COM2? _____

COM3? _____

COM4? _____

Step 7   Every tech should know what the default system resource settings are for COM and LPT ports. Compare the COM and LPT settings in the following table to the settings on your system, then commit the chart to memory.

Port	I/O Address	IRQ
COM1	3F8	4
COM2	2F8	3
LPT1	378	7
LPT2	278	5

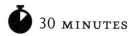 30 MINUTES

Lab Exercise 5.03: Installing Expansion Cards

There are five steps to installing any expansion card device properly:

1. Arm yourself with knowledge of the device before you install it. Is the device certified to run on the Windows OS that you're running? Is it compatible with your motherboard and other hardware? If you're using Windows NT/2000/XP, be certain to check the Hardware Compatibility List (HCL) before you do anything. The HCL is the definitive authority on which devices are guaranteed to work on these operating systems.

2. Remove the cover from your PC case and install the device. As always, follow all ESD and safety precautions, and handle the card with care.

3. Assign system resources to the device. In approximately 99.73% of the cases (a rough estimate), you'll never have to do this because PnP takes care of it for you, but if you're mixing old components with new, then you may have to assign resources manually to accommodate the old, non-PnP device.

4. Install device drivers for the component. Windows comes with many device drivers preinstalled, so it may try to help you by installing the driver that it thinks the device needs. In most cases, you should instead install updated drivers from the device manufacturer.

5. Verify that the device is functional and that it's not creating any conflicts with other devices on your system.

The exercise listed below is a somewhat abridged version of this procedure, because instead of installing a new device, you'll remove and reinstall devices that are already on your system.

✔ **Cross-Reference**

To review the details of device installation, refer to the "Installing Expansion Cards" section of Chapter 5 of *Mike Meyers' A+ Guide to PC Hardware*.

Learning Objectives

In this lab, you'll practice removing and installing internal expansion cards.

At the end of this lab, you'll be able to

- Remove and install expansion cards in a system correctly and safely

Lab Materials and Setup

The materials you need for this lab are

- At least one working computer with expansion cards installed
- Screwdriver
- Anti-static mat and wrist strap
- Anti-static storage bags
- Notepad

✔ **Hint**

As usual, if you have access to more than one system, take advantage of it.

Getting Down to Business

In this exercise, you'll physically remove expansion card devices from your PC. You'll then make note of any important information you can find on the device's label (device maker, version, and so on), and then reassemble and restart the system.

Shut down the system and unplug the power cable, then place it on your anti-static mat. Remove the PC case cover and strap on your anti-static wrist strap, and you're ready to start.

Step 1 Check your notes from Lab Exercise 5.01 and draw a sketch showing which device is installed in which slot on the motherboard.

Step 2 Remove the cards one at a time from your system. For each card, follow these procedures:

a) Remove the retaining screw and store it safely.

✔ **Hint**

You'll see two main types of screws used in PCs. On first glance, they may look all the same, but although these screws are the same overall size, they have different sizes of threads. Screws with the larger threads, commonly called *coarse-threaded* screws, are generally used to secure expansion cards, power supplies, and case covers. Screws with the smaller threads, commonly called *fine-threaded* screws, are typically used to secure storage devices such as hard drives, floppy disk drives, and CD media drives into their respective bays.

---

b) Taking hold of the card by its edges, carefully and firmly pull it straight up and out of its slot.

✔ **Hint**

These cards can be difficult to remove. If a card seems stuck, try rocking it back and forth (from front to back in the direction of the slot, not side to side).

---

c) Holding the card only by the edges and the metal flange, place it in an electrostatic bag for safekeeping.

Step 3 Examine each of the cards you removed from your system and record the pertinent information in your notebook.

Do any of the cards have writing or labels on them? If so, what information do these labels provide?

Can you identify the manufacturers of the cards? List each card with its manufacturer.

_____

_____

Are there any version numbers or codes on the cards? List this information for each card.

_____

_____

If there are there jumpers or DIP switches on any of the cards, how are they set? You might want to make a quick drawing of the switches and their current positions.

_____

Can you locate a "key" that shows you how to set the jumpers or DIP switches? If so, make a note about where you found this key—was it in the instruction manual, or perhaps printed directly on the expansion card circuit board?

_____

_____

Step 4 Reinstall the expansion cards you removed back into your system. For each card, follow these procedures:

a) Check your notes to confirm where to reinstall the card.

b) Align the card over its motherboard slot, making sure that the metal flange is aligned properly with the case slot. Holding the flange with one hand, place the heel of your hand on the top edge of the card and push the card firmly into the expansion slot.

c) Once the card is in the slot and the flange is flush with the case, replace the screw that holds the card in place.

Step 5 Restart your PC and use Device Manager to confirm that each device is working properly. If there is a missing driver, you'll see a yellow circle with a black exclamation point next to the device listing. If there is a resource conflict, the problem device will be disabled and a red X will appear next to its listing.

Lab Analysis Test

1. One of the systems at your client's graphics firm is an older AT-style system. It has a 700 MHz CPU, 512 MB of RAM, and a 32 MB AGP graphics card, and is running Windows 2000 Professional. It has one PCI and one ISA slot available. Can it be upgraded to accommodate the remaining requirements?

_____

_____

2. John has a system that runs at 2.4 GHz and uses a 64 MB AGP video card. He uses Windows XP Professional and wants to try its multiple-monitor support feature. Can he add another AGP video card?

_____

_____

3. Steve has a legacy ISA sound card on his system. The sound card uses I/O addresses 300–330 and IRQ 5. He installs an NIC and restarts the PC, which proceeds to lock up completely. What is most likely the problem?

_____

_____

4. Ellen opened her computer case and installed a PCI card to add a second parallel port for a printer. What IRQ will this card most likely use?

_____

_____

5. You've installed a NIC and a PCI FireWire controller card on Susan's Windows XP Professional system. The system starts up fine, but when you check Device Manager, you see a yellow circle with a black exclamation mark beside the NIC icon. What is the problem?

_____

_____

Key Term Quiz

Use the following vocabulary terms to complete the following sentences. Not all of the terms will be used.

AGP

DMA

expansion card

IEEE 1394 (FireWire)

I/O address

IRQ

ISA

PCI

system resources

USB

memory address

1. Most modern motherboards provide several _____ slots.

2. Modern video cards use the _____ slot.

3. The LPT1 port generally uses the default setting of 378 for its _____.

4. COM1 and COM3 share the same _____ setting of 4.

5. It's common for modern systems to provide at least two external _____ ports for adding peripheral devices.

Chapter 6

Motherboards

Lab Exercises

With all due respect to the CPU, system RAM, power supply, hard disk drive, and all the other sundry pieces of a typical PC, the motherboard is the real workhorse of the system. Every component on the PC plugs into the motherboard either directly or indirectly. Every bit and byte of data that moves between devices passes through the motherboard's sockets and traces. The motherboard is what brings all of the individual parts of the PC into a working whole. As such, replacing a motherboard is one of the most challenging of a PC techs' tasks. Luckily, there are only a couple of circumstances that require you to undertake this chore. The first, of course, is when the motherboard malfunctions or is damaged. Modern motherboards aren't made to be repaired, but rather to be replaced as a whole unit when they go bad. The other is when you wish to upgrade the PC to a more powerful CPU than its current motherboard supports.

In either of these cases, you've got a bit of work ahead of you. Installing a motherboard requires more effort than any other type of installation— more preparation, more time performing the installation, and more cleanup afterwards. Regardless of this, there is really no need to be intimidated by the prospect of replacing a motherboard. Motherboard installation is a common and necessary part of PC repair. In this chapter, you'll go through the process.

In the following exercises, you'll make preparations for a motherboard installation, including identifying the proper motherboard form factor, labeling cables and connectors, and then removing the motherboard from a working PC. You'll then write down notes about key motherboard features and finally, you'll reinstall the motherboard.

 30 MINUTES

Lab Exercise 6.01: Identifying Motherboard Form Factors

You're consulting for a small graphics firm that is upgrading their PCs to accommodate a major software upgrade and network restructuring. While assessing their PC stock, you discovered that a number of their systems lack sufficient CPU power to run their new CAD program. To remedy this, you must replace the motherboards of these systems with models that support newer and faster CPUs.

To be able to determine which of your client's systems need upgrading for the new CAD software, you have to be comfortable identifying motherboard types. PC motherboards come in two styles, or *form factors*: AT (including Baby AT) and ATX (including microATX and FlexATX). AT motherboards are the older style and are relatively rare these days. ATX motherboards are what you find in most PCs on the market.

Your first task when replacing motherboards is to determine which form factor each PC requires. As a rule, system cases are made for *either* AT *or* ATX motherboards; because of the differences in size and screw placement, you can't put an ATX motherboard in an AT case, and vice-versa. In a real-world situation, it would be a very exceptional situation where you'd actually try to upgrade an AT system.

Learning Objectives

In this lab, you'll become familiar with different motherboard layouts.

At the end of this lab, you'll be able to

- Recognize different motherboard form factors

- Understand considerations for upgrading a system with a newer motherboard

Lab Materials and Setup

The materials you need for this lab are

- If possible, one system with an ATX motherboard and a second with an AT motherboard, but at least one complete, working system

- Anti-static mat

- Anti-static wrist strap

✔ **Hint**

As usual, if you have access to multiple systems, take advantage of it. It's most useful to have a variety of motherboards to study.

Getting Down to Business

We'll start this exercise with a review of the characteristics of the two motherboard form factors, and then open up your PC case to determine what type of motherboard is installed. Shut down your PC, disconnect the power cable from the wall socket, and place the case on its side on your anti-static mat, then perform the following steps.

✔ **Cross-Reference**

> To refresh your recollection on motherboard types, refer to the "Types of Motherboards" section of Chapter 6 of *Mike Meyers' A+ Guide to PC Hardware*.

Step 1   Answer the following questions, referring back to the textbook chapter as needed:

What are four characteristics that differentiate an ATX motherboard from an AT motherboard?

_____

_____

_____

_____

What is the physical size difference between an ATX motherboard and a microATX motherboard?

_____

_____

Can you replace a Full AT motherboard with a Baby AT motherboard?

_____

_____

Step 2   Look on the back panel of your PC case to answer the following questions:

Does your PC use a DIN or mini DIN keyboard connector?

_____

Are the serial, parallel, and USB connector ports on a single panel near the keyboard connector, or on separate dongle flanges?

_____

_____

Based on the answers to the questions above, what can you tell about the type of motherboard form factor your PC uses?

_____

_____

_____

Step 3 Remove the case cover from your PC to answer the following questions:

Does your PC use a single P1 power connector or a pair of P8/P9 connectors?

_____

_____

Does the main power switch plug into the motherboard or does a cable run from the power switch directly to the power supply?

_____

_____

Based on the answers to the questions above, what can you tell about the type of motherboard form factor your PC uses?

_____

_____

_____

Replace the PC case cover, but since the next lab exercise requires you to access the inside of your PC case, leave it unplugged and turned off.

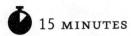 15 MINUTES

Lab Exercise 6.02: Removing and Labeling Components and Cables

Once you've selected those of your client's systems that will need new motherboards, you can't just rip the old ones out. To get to the motherboard, you have to first remove the installed expansion cards and cables. Many of us have had the experience of taking something apart only to wind up with leftover parts after we put it back together. To avoid this result when you disassemble a PC, you should get into the habit of properly storing and labeling any parts that you remove from the system. This includes everything from the major components to the screws that hold them in place and the cables that connect them to the motherboard.

✔ **Hint**

Of course, you don't need to attach a label to each individual screw, but do keep them organized in labeled containers to avoid confusion!

Learning Objectives

In this lab, you'll remove and label expansion card components, cables, and connectors in preparation for removing the motherboard.

At the end of this lab, you'll be able to

- Remove and label expansion cards
- Remove and label data cables and connectors
- Remove and label power cables

Lab Materials and Setup

The materials you need for this lab are

- A working computer
- Its motherboard manual or online documentation
- Post-It notes and a pen
- Screwdriver
- Anti-static mat
- Anti-static wrist strap
- Anti-static bags

Getting Down to Business

Starting with your system shut down, remove the PC cover case and strap on your anti-static wrist strap. Have your labeling materials handy and follow the steps listed below:

Step 1 Following the procedure laid out in Lab Exercise 5.03 in the previous chapter, remove any expansion cards from the PC, label each one with a Post-it note that identifies the card, and store it in an anti-static bag.

Step 2   Disconnect and label the following data cables:

- Hard disk drives

- CD-or DVD-media disk drives

- Floppy disk drive

- Sound (this cable runs from the CD-or DVD-media disk drive to the sound card)

- Parallel connector dongle (AT motherboards only)

- Serial connector dongle (AT motherboards only)

- USB connector dongle (AT motherboards only)

Step 3   Disconnect and label the following power cables:

- Hard disk drives

- CD- or DVD-media disk drives

- Floppy disk drive

- CPU fan

- Motherboard (P1 on ATX motherboards, P8/P9 on AT motherboards)

- Case-mounted power switch (AT motherboards only)

Step 4   Disconnect and label the front panel control wires (also called the *harness wires*) from the motherboard. Be certain to use the motherboard manual to properly label these wires! Front panel control wires typically include the power button (on ATX motherboards), reset button, front panel LEDs (power, hard disk activity, and so on), and system speaker.

✔ Hint

To label wires, use the small Post-its, or cut the square ones into strips. Fold the sticky part of the Post-It over the wire and stick it to the back to make a tag you can write on.

Step 5   Depending on your system, you may have to remove other devices to ensure that you have sufficient clearance to lift the motherboard out of the PC case in the next exercise. Visually confirm whether any components block an easy removal path. Are any hard disk drives or CD- or DVD-media disk drives in the way? Is the power supply in the way? Make certain that you remove anything against which you could bump the motherboard, RAM, or CPU fan during removal.

 15 MINUTES

Lab Exercise 6.03: Removing a Motherboard

With all of your PC components and cables safely tucked away, the next step in your upgrade job is to remove the old motherboards so they can be replaced. Techs will tell you that motherboard removal is the exercise that separates the geek from the meek and the true PC tech from the wannabe, but don't let that intimidate you! Motherboard removal is completely straightforward and simple.

Learning Objectives

In this lab, you'll remove your PC's motherboard.

At the end of this lab, you'll be able to

- Remove a motherboard safely and correctly

Lab Materials and Setup

The materials you need for this lab are

- A working computer on which you've performed Lab Exercise 6.02
- Screwdriver
- Anti-static mat and anti-static wrist strap
- A large anti-static bag

Getting Down to Business

Following the same ESD procedures listed in the previous exercises, you'll now remove the mounting screws for the motherboard and lift it out of the PC case.

Step 1 Locate and remove the screws holding the motherboard to the frame of the case. There are most likely six to nine screws, which may also have small washers. Be sure not to lose these washers, as they help prevent overtightening the screws. Some systems may use small plastic supports called *stand-offs* between the motherboard and the frame. Remove these and store them in a labeled container.

> ✖ **Warning**
>
> Remember to handle the motherboard as you would any printed circuit board: gently, by the edges, as if you were holding a delicate old photograph.

Step 2 Carefully remove the motherboard from the PC case and place it on your anti-static mat. You should place the motherboard in a large anti-static bag for the best protection.

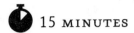 15 MINUTES

Lab Exercise 6.04: Identifying Motherboard Features

At a glance, one motherboard pretty much looks like another. Of course, as a PC tech, you know that this isn't true: two identical-looking motherboards can easily have completely different feature sets. Chipsets, bus speed, CPU socket type, clock speed, and so on are just some of the important features that separate one motherboard from another. These differences don't always make themselves obvious, so once again you need to turn to your motherboard manual to identify your motherboard's features, as described in the following steps.

Learning Objectives

In this lab, you'll become familiar with different motherboard features.

At the end of this lab, you'll be able to

- Recognize different motherboard features
- Identify the location of motherboard features

Lab Materials and Setup

The materials you need for this lab are

- A motherboard, such as the one you removed in Lab Exercise 6.03
- The motherboard manual or online documentation for that motherboard

Getting Down to Business

In the following steps, you'll identify the location of key features on your motherboard.

✔ **Hint**

If you're using the motherboard you removed in the previous lab, take this opportunity to clean any dust off it using canned air before you begin.

Step 1   Note the location of the make and model information on the motherboard in Figure 6-1. Compare this to your motherboard and locate the manufacturer name and model number.

✔ **Cross-Reference**

For details on chipsets, refer to the "Chipset Varieties" section of Chapter 6 of *Mike Meyers' A+ Guide to PC Hardware.*

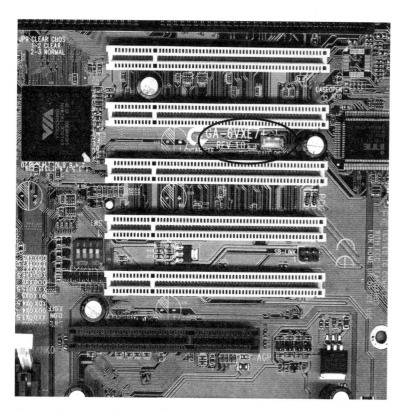

Figure 6-1 A motherboard's model number can be hard to spot.

What is the name of your motherboard manufacturer? _____

What is the model number of your motherboard? _____

What type of chipset do you have on your motherboard? _____

Keep this information handy! Having the make and model of your motherboard readily available makes it easy to search the web for drivers and updated BIOS.

Step 2 Look for any charts or numbers printed on the surface of the motherboard:

What are the settings for the motherboard speed? _____

What are the settings for the CPU timings? _____

What are the settings for the CPU voltages? _____

Step 3 Which of the following ways can you use to set the CPU speed and clock ratio?

Jumpers _____

DIP switches _____

CMOS _____

Step 4   Locate the following on your motherboard.

- System clock battery

- BIOS

- Chipset (Northbridge/Southbridge)

 30 MINUTES

Lab Exercise 6.05: Installing a Motherboard

Now that you've removed the old inadequate motherboards from your client's systems, you get to the *real* test of your tech skills: installing the new motherboards and reconnecting everything so that the computers work! Once again, however, there's no need to be intimidated. Everything you need to install a motherboard (in your case, probably the motherboard you just removed in Lab Exercise 6.03) is right in front of you, so let's get started.

Learning Objectives

In this lab, you'll install a motherboard. You can use the motherboard and system you disassembled in Lab Exercise 6.03.

At the end of this lab, you'll be able to

- Install a PC motherboard and connect all its associated components

Lab Materials and Setup

The materials you need for this lab are

- A working system from which the motherboard has been removed

- Components and cables previously connected to the removed motherboard

- Motherboard manual or online documentation for the motherboard

- Anti-static mat

- Anti-static wrist strap

- Notepad and pen

Getting Down to Business

Physically installing the motherboard itself is mostly a matter of being careful and methodical. The more complex part of the task is reattaching all the cables and cards in their proper places.

✖ Warning

Motherboards are full of delicate electronics! Remember to follow the proper ESD and safety procedures.

✔ Hint

When installing a motherboard, it's handy to use your notepad to check off assembly steps as you go along.

Step 1 Carefully line up the motherboard inside the PC case and secure it in place with the mounting screws. Be sure to use the washers and plastic standoffs (if supplied).

Step 2 Insert the front panel control wires in their appropriate places. These should include your power button (on ATX motherboards), reset button, front panel LEDs (power, hard disk activity, and so on), system speaker, and so on. Refer to the labels and your motherboard documentation for the proper connections.

Step 3 Connect all power cables. These include the hard disk drives, CD-or DVD-media disk drives, floppy disk drive, CPU fan, main motherboard, and so on. On AT systems, you'll also need to connect the case-mounted power switch.

Step 4 Connect all data cables. These include the hard disk drives, CD- or DVD-media drives, floppy disk drive, sound cable, and on AT motherboards, the cables for the parallel, serial, and USB connector dongles.

Step 5 Install the expansion card components.

Step 6 Now comes perhaps the most important step—double-check *all* of your connections and cards to make sure that they're properly seated and connected where they're supposed to be! If something is out of whack, it's definitely better to discover it now than later after you've hit the power switch.

Step 7 Finally, if you're using the PC you previously disassembled, now you may replace the case cover on your PC, plug the keyboard, mouse, and monitor back in, and then plug the power cable back in and turn it on. Assuming you've done everything correctly, your system will boot up normally.

Lab Analysis Test

1. John tried to use an old (but working!) AT power supply he had lying around to replace a dead ATX power supply in his system, but he couldn't plug it in. Why?

   _____

   _____

2. Keith bought a new fancy case for his system. He removed the motherboard from his old case, but discovered it wouldn't fit in the new one. What did Keith forget to check?

   _____

   _____

3. Dianne is trying to install an AT motherboard in a new, empty AT case. She tries to set it down in the bottom of the case, but it won't fit—the ports on the side are too low to poke out the back of the case, and she can't make the screws work at all. What has she forgotten?

   _____

   _____

4. After Joe reassembled his PC and turned it on, he noticed that the green LED and the disk active LED never light up but everything seems to work okay. What is the problem?

   _____

   _____

5. John wants to upgrade his system by replacing the CPU. His friend has offered him a Pentium 4 chip he has extra. John's current CPU is a Pentium P166. Will this work? Why or why not?

   _____

   _____

Key Term Quiz

Use the following vocabulary terms to complete the following sentences. Not all of the terms will be used.

AT

ATX

chipset

motherboard manual

P1 power connector

P8/P9 power connector

1. The power supplies for modern ATX motherboards connect using the _____.

2. To check the technical specifications of a motherboard, consult its _____.

3. PS/2 connectors are found on _____ motherboards.

4. The Northbridge and Southbridge are components of a motherboard's _____.

5. DIN connectors are found on _____ motherboards.

Chapter 7

Power Supplies

Lab Exercises

The term "power supply" can be misleading. The power supply in a PC does not supply power; it just takes the alternating current (AC) supplied by the power company and transforms it to the direct current (DC) used by the computer system. Local power companies supply AC to the outlet in your home or office. Some conversion must take place to supply the lower operating voltages and DC required for the PC to function.

A technician must understand the difference between AC and DC power. You must be able to measure the AC power at the wall outlet to determine if it is correct and if the three wires are properly connected. You must also measure the DC output of the power supply inside the PC case to determine whether the power supply is providing the correct DC voltage.

The power supply in a PC is an electronic device that converts the higher voltage AC—120 volts (V) in the United States or 240 V outside the United States—into the three power levels of 12 V, 5 V, and 3.3 V DC used in today's PC systems. The 12 V have been traditionally used for devices that have motors to spin, such as hard drives, floppy drives, CD-ROM drives, fans, and so on. The 5 Vs and 3.3 V support all of the onboard electronics.

Two types of power supplies make up the majority of all PC power supplies installed: AT and ATX. AT form factor computers are fading away, but their huge installed base requires you to recognize and understand the AT power supply. More important, the A+ exam assumes you understand both the AT and the ATX power supplies.

Let's assume that a client calls you saying that her PC keeps locking up. After walking her through a few simple troubleshooting steps, you rule out a virus or a misbehaving application. This leaves hardware as the possible culprit; in all likelihood, it's the power supply. In these lab exercises, you'll practice the procedures for measuring power going to the PC, testing the PC's power supply, and replacing a PC power supply.

✔ **Hint**

The A+ Core Hardware exam really shows its American roots in the area of electrical power. Watch for power questions that discuss American power standards—especially ones related to household voltage and outlet plug design.

 30 MINUTES

Lab Exercise 7.01: Electricity

Troubleshooting power-related problems is one of the trickier tasks you'll undertake as a PC tech. Your first step is to go right to the source, so to speak, and make certain that the power being supplied to the PC from the electrical outlet is good.

✔ **Cross-Reference**

For details on AC power from the power company, refer to the "Securing AC" section of Chapter 7 of *Mike Meyers' A+ Guide to PC Hardware*.

✖ **Warning**

In a classroom, you have the benefit of an instructor to show you how to do these exercises the first time. If you're doing these on your own with no experience, seek the advice of a trained technician or instructor.

Learning Objectives

At the end of this lab, you'll be able to

- Determine if the AC wiring is correct at a wall outlet
- Determine if the AC voltages are correct at a wall outlet

Lab Materials and Setup

The materials you need for this lab are

- An AC electrical outlet tester
- A multimeter

Getting Down to Business

Measuring the voltage coming from an AC outlet is a nerve-wracking task even for experienced techs! Sticking objects into a live power outlet goes against everything we've been taught since infancy, but when done properly it really is completely safe.

Be sure to use common sense and appropriate safety procedures. If you're not familiar with using a multimeter, please review the course materials or ask your instructor for a demonstration.

✔ **Hint**

If a PC is having unexplained errors and you suspect the power supply, don't be too hasty in replacing it. First check the wall outlet. Older buildings are known to have bad wiring in them. By "bad," I mean connected improperly or providing poor power.

Step 1   Look at Figure 7-1, and compare it to your electrical outlet.

A typical electrical socket has three openings: hot, neutral, and ground. The hot wire delivers the juice. The neutral wire acts as a drain and returns electricity to the local source (the breaker panel). The semi-rounded ground socket returns excess electricity to the ground. If your outlet doesn't have a ground socket—and many older buildings don't—then don't use it—ungrounded outlets aren't appropriate for PCs.

✖ **Warning!**

Take all appropriate safety precautions before measuring live electrical outlets.

Figure 7-1 A typical AC electrical outlet

FIGURE 7-2 A circuit tester
for AC electrical outlets

Step 2   Determine whether or not your electrical socket is "live." Do this with your electrical outlet
tester. Plug your outlet tester (see Figure 7-2) into the electrical outlet or power strip where you plug in
the PC. Look at the LED indicators. Are they showing good power?

Step 3   Measure the voltage in the 120 V AC circuit by inserting the two multimeter probes into the hot
and neutral openings of the outlet. Set your multimeter to AC voltage. Do not proceed until you're sure
you have done this correctly! If you aren't sure, ask your instructor for guidance. Referring to Figure 7-3,
take the black probe and place it in the neutral opening of the wall socket. Make sure you have good contact inside the outlet. The metal probe tip must contact the metal connector inside the outlet.

Next, place the red probe inside the hot opening. Again, you must make good metal-to-metal contact. You may have to reposition the probes you get a good reading for the AC circuit. Your reading
should be somewhere between 110 and 120 V.

What is your reading? _____

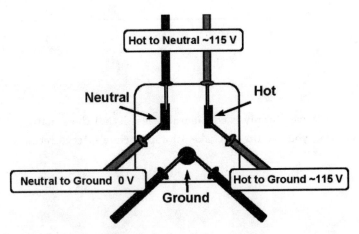

FIGURE 7-3 Multimeter probe locations when testing an AC outlet

Step 4   Measure the voltage in the hot-to-ground circuit. Take the black probe, and place it into the ground opening of the outlet (refer to Figure 7-3). Make sure you have good contact. Take the red probe, and place it into the hot opening. Move the probes around until you get a good reading for the AC voltage. Again, your reading should be in the 110 to 120 V range.

What is your reading? _____

Step 5   The last measurement you need to make is the voltage in the neutral-to-ground safety circuit. When the neutral wire is broken or missing, the ground wire is the only way for wayward electrons to depart safely. Any electricity on both the neutral and ground wires should have a direct path back to earth, so there should be *no* voltage between these wires.

Place the black probe into the ground opening of the outlet. Make sure you have good contact. Place the red probe into the neutral opening. Move the probes around until you get a good reading for the AC voltage. You should get a reading of 0 V.

What is your reading? _____

Step 6   Measure another outlet in the same building, and repeat the previous steps. Are the readings similar? If the readings from your electrical are outside of the ranges described, it's time to call an electrician. Assuming your reading is showing good power, go to the next exercise.

 30 MINUTES

Lab Exercise 7.02: Power Supply Output

Once you've determined that the AC power going to your client's PC is good, the next troubleshooting step is to test whether the DC power traveling from the power supply to the rest of her system is good.

✔ **Cross-Reference**

For details on DC power from the power supply, refer to the "Supplying DC" section of Chapter 7 of *Mike Meyers' A+ Guide to PC Hardware.*

✖ **Warning**

Although the power coming out of the PC power supply is considerably less lethal than that coming directly out of the electrical outlet, you should still take all appropriate safety precautions before taking measurements.

Learning Objectives

At the end of this lab, you'll be able to

- Identify the connectors of a PC power supply

- Measure the output of a PC power supply

Lab Materials and Setup

The materials you need for this lab are

- A working PC with an AT or ATX power supply

- A multimeter

Getting Down to Business

In the following steps, you'll measure DC voltage coming from the PC power supply. The two places to measure power supply output are at the Molex power connectors and at the motherboard power connector. Molex power connectors plug into devices that need 5 or 12 volts of power. These include hard disk drives and CD- or DVD-media drives. Mini connectors also carry 5 or 12 volts, but on modern systems are only used for floppy disk drives. If you're using a Pentium 4 PC, your power supply may also have a connector like the one shown in Figure 7-4. This is the new ATX12V (also called a P4) connector used on motherboards requiring an additional 12 V supply.

Motherboard power connectors come in two flavors: the newer ATX motherboards use the single P1 connector, while AT motherboards use the dual P8/P9 connectors.

Step 1   Set the multimeter to read DC voltage. Find a Molex connector that's not being used for a device. If no Molex connectors are unused, turn the system off and disconnect the one from the CD- or DVD-media drive. Now, turn the PC back on.

Step 2   Referring to Figure 7-5, place the black probe into either one of the holes on the Molex connector that is aligned with a black wire. Now place the red probe into each of the other three holes of the Molex connector in turn, first the other black wire, then the red, then yellow, and record your findings.

Black wire to black wire   _____ V

Black wire to red wire   _____ V

Black wire to yellow wire   _____ V

Figure 7-4 A P4 connector

Step 3 Measuring the voltage from the motherboard connector is a little trickier. Leave the power connector plugged into the motherboard and push the probes into the end of the connector that the wires run into. You must push the probe deep enough to touch the metal contact pins, but be careful not to push too deeply or you might push the pin out of the connector.

Push the black probe into the motherboard connector alongside any black wire, and leave it there. Insert the red probe into each of the other wires, and record your findings. Depending on your motherboard connector, you may not have all these wires.

Black wire to red wire   _____ V

Black wire to yellow wire   _____ V

Black wire to purple wire   _____ V

Black wire to white wire   _____ V

Black wire to black wire   _____ V

Black wire to blue wire   _____ V

Black wire to green wire   _____ V

✔ **Hint**

The voltages generated by the power supply must be within a tolerance (range) level; readings outside these ranges mean the power supply should be replaced. 5 V connections have a tolerance of +/-2 percent (4.9 to 5.1 V is okay), and 12 V connections have a tolerance of +/-6 percent (11.25 to 12.75 V is okay).

FIGURE 7-5 Measuring the voltage in a Molex connector

> ✔ **Hint**
>
> A single reading from your power supply may not be enough to pinpoint a power-related problem. Sometimes a power problem only becomes evident when the power supply is placed under a heavier-than-normal load, such as burning CDs. Also, some RAM-related errors mimic a failing power supply.

 30 MINUTES

Lab Exercise 7.03: Replacing a Power Supply

Let's assume that you've found a variance in the 12 V range that explains your client's system lockups. You know that power supplies aren't user-serviceable components—you don't fix them, you replace them as a unit—so it's time to replace her power supply. Next to the motherboard, the power supply is the most time-consuming component to replace, simply because of all the dang wires! Nonetheless, replacing the power supply is a simple operation, as described below.

Learning Objectives

At the end of this lab, you'll be able to

- Determine the correct size of power supply for the system
- Replace a power supply

Lab Materials and Setup

The materials you need for this lab are

- A working PC with an AT or ATX power supply
- A screwdriver
- A labeled container for holding screws

Getting Down to Business

One of the areas where PC manufacturers cut corners on lower-end systems is power supplies. High-end systems typically come with higher-wattage power supplies, whereas entry-level PCs typically have lower-wattage power supplies. This might not be evident until you add power-hungry components to the system, which places a heavier load on the power supply causing an early failure.

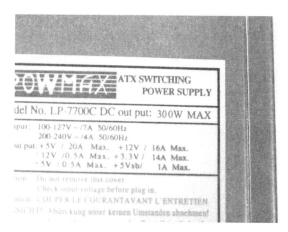

FIGURE 7-6 Typical ATX power supply ratings label

In the following steps you'll determine the wattage of the power supply on your system, calculate the power usage of your PC, and then remove and reinstall the power supply.

Step 1   Let's find out what the wattage rating of your power supply is. Look at the label on the power supply in Figure 7-6.

Find the similar label on your power supply, and locate the watts rating. If you don't see something like the "300 W" on the label in Figure 7-6, the power supply rating may be hidden in the model number, such as ATXPS-250.

✔ **Hint**

All power supplies have a wattage rating. If it is not apparent on the power supply itself, search the Internet using the model number for reference.

What is the wattage of your power supply? _____

Step 2   When it comes time to replace a power supply, don't skimp on the wattage! Modern power supplies typically range from 200 watts to 600 watts. 200-watt power supplies are the bare minimum you would use on a system that has only a few installed components (such as a single hard disk drive and CD- or DVD-media drive), while the 600-watt models are usually found on server systems that have multiple hard disk drives (such as a RAID array) or other power-hungry components. As a rule of thumb, get the highest-wattage replacement you can afford while maintaining compatibility with your system.

✖ **Warning**

Never replace a PC's power supply with one of lower wattage!

Use the following table to calculate the overall wattage needed for your system. Add the numbers for each component and determine the lowest and highest wattage requirements.

Component	Requirement	Voltage(s) Used
AGP video card	30–50 W	3.3 V
PCI card	5–10 W	5 V
10/100 NIC	4 W	3.3 V
SCSI controller PCI	20 W	3.3 V and 5 V
Floppy drive	5 W	5 V
7200 rpm IDE hard drive	5–20 W	5 V and 12 V
10,000 rpm SCSI drive	10–40 W	5 V and 12 V
CD/DVD media drive	10–25 W	5 V and 12 V
Case/CPU fans	3 W (each)	12 V
Motherboard (without CPU or RAM)	25–40 W	3.3 V and 5 V
RAM	10 W per 128 MB	3.3 V
Pentium III processor	38 W	5 V
Pentium 4 processor	70 W	12 V
AMD Athlon processor	70 W	12 V

If the highest total exceeds the power supply wattage rating, you may run into problems. When selecting a new power supply, you should multiply the load by a factor of 1.5. The multiplier provides a safety factor and allows the power supply to run more efficiently. Power supplies are more efficient at 30 to 70 percent of their full capacity rating. Thus, a 300 W supply works best when only 90 to 210 watts are being used.

What wattage is appropriate for your system? _____

✔ **Hint**

Depending on the design of your PC case, you may have to remove data cables or components in order to get to the power supply. Make certain that you have plenty of room to work inside the case!

Step 3 Shut down the system and remove the power cable from the back of the power supply. Then remove the power supply.

   a) Disconnect the Molex and Mini connectors from your drive devices, then unplug the main power connector from the motherboard.

   b) If your power supply uses a P4 connector, disconnect it from the motherboard.

c) If using an AT power supply, disconnect the main power switch from the PC case.

d) Unscrew the four screws holding the power supply onto the case (remembering to support it while you remove the last one!) and remove the power supply from the PC case. Store the screws in the labeled container.

Step 4 Take this opportunity to inspect and clean the power supply. Check for any rust or corrosion on the power supply casing or on any of the contacts. Inspect the wires for damage or frayed insulation. Use canned air to blow dust and dirt out of the intake and exhaust vents.

Step 5 Reinstall the power supply by performing the installation steps in reverse order. If you had to remove data cables or other components to get at the power supply, be sure to reattach them.

 30 MINUTES

Lab Exercise 7.04: Power Protection

You've successfully fixed your client's power-problem-plagued PC (say *that* five times fast!), but now you've noted that she has nothing in the way of power protection for her system, nor do any of her coworkers. None!

When you mention it to her, she tells you that her boss never really saw the point of spending money on surge protectors, uninterruptible power supplies, or any of "that stuff." With a straight face, she asks, "Do those things really do any good?"

Now it's your task to sell the boss on the idea of power protection. To do this, you must explain the types of power problems that lurk in the bushes just waiting to pounce on unwary users without power protection, and suggest precautions that they can take to prevent power-related damage.

Learning Objectives

At the end of this lab, you'll be able to

- Explain the need for power protection
- Explain the types of power protection available for a PC

✔ **Cross-Reference**

For details on power protection, refer to the "UPS" and "Surge Suppressors" sections of Chapter 7 of *Mike Meyers' A+ Guide to PC Hardware*.

Lab Materials and Setup

The materials you need for this lab are

- A working PC

Getting Down to Business

Too often, PC users take the electricity that powers their system for granted. After all, there's not much you can do about the electricity, is there? Not so! Armed with the knowledge of the types of power conditions that can affect your PC, you can then determine what precautions to take.

Step 1 Describe the following types of power conditions and the type of damage they can cause:

Power spike

_____

_____

Brownout

_____

_____

Blackout

_____

_____

Step 2 Describe the following types of power protection equipment:

Surge suppressor

_____

_____

Online uninterruptible power supply (UPS)

_____

_____

Standby UPS

_____

_____

Lab Analysis Test

1. Your client calls you and says that her PC is unusually quiet and keeps rebooting for no apparent reason. What should you ask her to check?

_____

_____

2. Athena lives in an area where the power is often interrupted. She bought a good surge protector strip, but that does not seem to help. What does she need to prevent her system from shutting down unexpectedly?

_____

_____

3. Your assistant technician calls you and says he suspects a bad power supply in one of your client's system. He said the multimeter readings are 12.65 and 4.55. What should he do?

_____

_____

4. One of your clients has an older Pentium III system with a single IDE hard disk drive and 512MB of RAM. He has been using this PC as his main workstation, but has purchased a newer system and now wants to redeploy the older system as a file server on his network. He has ordered a PCI SCSI controller board and three SCSI drives, so that he can configure a RAID array, and an additional 2 GB of RAM. He also ordered two Y adapters for the power supply connectors. He asks for your advice about any additional hardware he should order. What do you tell him?

_____

_____

5. What are the power requirements of the following system? _____

- AMD Athlon CPU and 256 MB RAM
- Two Enhanced Integrated Drive Electronics (EIDE) hard drives and one floppy drive
- One CD-RW drive and one DVD-ROM drive
- AGP video
- PCI, sound, and modem
- NIC

Key Term Quiz

Use the following vocabulary terms to complete the following sentences. Not all of the terms will be used.

12 V

5 V

Molex connector

P1

P4

P8/P9

power spikes

power supply

UPS

1. The AT form factor power supply plugs into the motherboard using the _____ connector(s)

2. PC devices with motors, such as hard drives, usually require _____ of power.

3. Hard drives and CD-ROMs connect to the power supply with a _____.

4. A surge protector prevents damage from _____ in the voltage.

5. Pentium 4 motherboards have both _____ and _____ power connectors.

Chapter 8

Floppy Drives

Lab Exercises

A floppy drive has the distinction of being the only component of a modern PC to contain basically the same technology as the original IBM PC. It's hard to believe, but when the first PCs came out, the entire data storage system consisted of a single floppy drive and multiple floppy disks holding a little more than 300,000 bytes of data each! Since those early days, there have been huge advances in storage technology, yet the PC industry continues to use floppy drives despite their ancient technology and tiny capacities.

Why do floppy drives persist? While storage devices called *hard drives* can contain billions of bytes of data, they can fail—in which case you'll still depend on the floppy drive, and a disk that can hold less than 2 million bytes of data, to help troubleshoot the system. Because floppy drives are still found on most systems, the A+ exams expect you to know how to deal with them.

The labs in this chapter prepare you for working with, installing, configuring, and troubleshooting floppy drives.

 30 MINUTES

Lab Exercise 8.01: Installing Floppy Drives

Your boss recently approved the purchase of a number of new workstations, all without floppy disk drives. (Apparently, the manufacturer of these workstations had decided that floppy drive technology was *passé*.) The employees assigned to the new machines have complained so much that the boss has decided to retrofit all the new workstations with 3.5-inch floppy drives. You have been assigned the task of adding floppy drives to these PCs.

✔ **Cross-Reference**

To review the details of floppy drive installation, refer to the "Installing Floppy Drives" section of Chapter 8 of *Mike Meyers' A+ Guide to PC Hardware*.

Learning Objectives

In this lab, you'll practice removing and installing a floppy drive.

At the end of this lab, you'll be able to

- Remove a floppy drive safely and correctly

- Install a floppy drive safely and correctly

Lab Materials and Setup

The materials you need for this lab are

- A working computer system with a floppy drive installed

- A known good floppy disk with data

Getting Down to Business

Although this lab starts with a working floppy disk drive installed in a PC—a likely scenario in a class-room setting—when building a system you'd obviously need to install one from scratch. On a new system, you'd start this lab at step 5.

Step 1 Begin with the PC system turned on and the standard Windows Desktop displayed. To verify that the floppy drive works, insert a known good floppy disk containing files into the drive and view the files on it by following these steps:

a)   Double-click the My Computer icon on the Desktop.

b)   Double-click the 3½ Floppy (A:) icon in the window (see Figure 8-1).

c)   Observe the files and folders displayed.

Do you see files displayed? _____

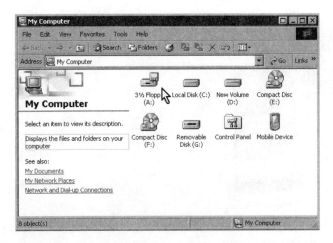

Figure 8-1 Accessing the contents of a floppy disk

✔ **Hint**

If no files are displayed, try another floppy disk. Also, be sure to insert the disk properly. You should hear a ratcheting sound when you double-click the floppy drive icon. This is the read mechanism opening the metal cover so it can read the data on the disk.

Step 2 Properly shut down the system, unplug the main power cable, and open the case following good ESD procedures.

Step 3 Carefully disconnect the two cables from the back of the floppy drive. One is the four-wire cable from the power supply (with its Mini connector), and the other is the flat ribbon cable that carries the data to and from the drive.

✖ **Warning**

Be sure to notice the seven-wire twist in the ribbon cable before you disconnect it. Is the twist closer to the drive or the motherboard? If you put this cable back on incorrectly, the floppy drive will not work. The end with the twist (see Figure 8-2) always goes to the floppy drive.

✔ **Hint**

If your lab has gone sleekly high tech and uses rounded data cables rather than the traditional flat ribbon cables, you can safely assume that the connector on the end will have a marking for the A: drive.

Floppy B

Floppy A

Floppy controller plug

FIGURE 8-2 The twist in one end of the floppy drive ribbon cable

Now disconnect the other end of the ribbon cable from the motherboard. These cables can be quite firmly attached to the motherboard, so use the following procedure: grab the connector, or grab as close to the connector as you can, and pull straight up firmly but gently. Sometimes a connector will seem to stick on one side—make sure that you don't pull unevenly, or you may bend the pins on the motherboard.

How many wires make up the ribbon cable? (Go ahead, count 'em!) _____

Is one of the wires a different color from the rest? _____

Why is it a different color? _____

Look at the motherboard where the cable was attached, and examine the pins.

How many pins do you count? _____

Look at the shape of the connection.

Is it symmetrical, meaning you can plug the connector in either direction, or is one side *keyed* to prevent you from inserting it backward? _____

Locate pin 1 (where the colored wire attaches) and pin 34.

The 34th pin is the drive change signal/disk change signal. It indicates when a disk has been physically changed. If this wire is broken or not connected, the system will read the initial disk placed in the floppy drive after power is applied and remember the contents for that disk, no matter how many times you change disks during a session, until you reboot the system.

Compare your motherboard connection for the floppy drive with the one shown in Figure 8-3.

Step 4 Remove the floppy drive from the case. There are so many different ways that floppy drives are held in system cases that it would be impossible to list all of the various carriers, caddies, bays, and so on that might be used to hold your floppy drive.

Almost all floppy drives are secured to these carriers, caddies, and bays with fine-threaded screws. The threads on these screws are narrower than those on the screws commonly used to secure expansion cards and the case cover. There should be two screws in each side of the floppy drive for support.

Figure 8-3 The orientation of the floppy drive connector on the motherboard

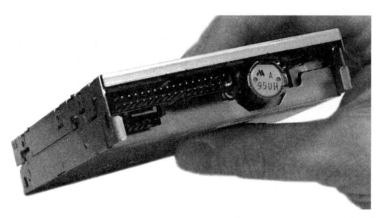

Figure 8-4 Examining the connections for the ribbon cable (top) and power cable (bottom) on the back of a floppy drive

✔ **Hint**

Get in the habit of storing screws safely while you're changing out or inspecting hardware. You can use a small plastic bowl, a coffee cup, or an empty baby food jar or breath mint tin—but if you let those screws roll around loose, you may not have enough of them the next time you need to install a device!

Step 5 Now that you have removed the floppy drive, inspect it. Look at the area where the cables connect (see Figure 8-4).

Is this ribbon cable area keyed or notched? _____

Find the indicator for the location of pin 1 on the floppy drive.

What and where is it? _____

On which side of the connector does the red orientation stripe of the cable go: toward the center or toward the outside? _____

How many physical pins are on your floppy drive? _____

Look at the area where the power is attached.

How many pins are there? _____

Experiment to see if you can insert the power connector incorrectly. Be gentle!

Can you connect it upside down? _____

Can you connect it without covering every pin? _____

On which side of the Mini connector does the red wire go: toward the center or toward the outside?

_____

It is possible to force the power connector on incorrectly, which will cause damage to the drive. Practice how it feels to make this connection properly and improperly, so that when you do it from an odd angle (for example, lying on your back under a desk), you know how it should feel.

Step 6   Reinstall the floppy drive by placing it back where you found it in the case. Be sure to use the proper fine-threaded screws to secure the floppy drive.

Now attach a Mini power connector to the floppy drive to provide power, and attach the 34-pin ribbon cable securely to the drive.

Attach the ribbon cable to the motherboard. Make sure it is secure and all the pins are covered.

Did you make sure that pin 1 was connected properly at both ends of the ribbon cable?

Are the connectors properly aligned so that pin 34 is connected on both ends of the cable?

Step 7   Once everything is back in place, leave the system cover off so that you can make adjustments if needed. Start the system, and watch the green LED on the front of the floppy drive.

If the green LED does not turn on at all during the boot process, then check your power connection.

If the green LED comes on and stays on all the time, then the ribbon cable is not connected properly.

Is everything working properly? _____

After you confirm that everything is working, place the cover back onto your system. Start Windows and test your floppy drive as you did in step 1 of this lab.

 30 MINUTES

Lab Exercise 8.02: Configuring Floppy Drives

A new client has very specific needs for the floppy disk drives in his computer center's seven computers. For the two servers, you'll need to install floppy drives, but disable them in CMOS. Three of the five workstations need the floppy drive set as the first drive in the boot sequence, but the other two need the CD-ROM drive to be first in the boot sequence, with the floppy drive second. You need to set up these PCs properly, so get to work!

For a refresher on the ins and outs of floppy drive configuration, refer to the "CMOS" section of Chapter 8 of *Mike Meyers' A+ Guide to PC Hardware*.

Learning Objectives

In this lab, you'll use the CMOS setup program to configure the floppy drive settings.

At the end of this lab, you'll be able to

- Locate the CMOS setup screens for configuring floppy drives
- Know the proper settings for configuring a floppy drive

Lab Materials and Setup

The materials you need for this lab are

- A working computer system with a floppy drive installed

Getting Down to Business

In Lab Exercise 8.01, you physically removed and reinstalled a floppy drive—but that's only half of the installation process. This lab exercise involves the floppy drive controller, and shows you how to configure the floppy drive in CMOS.

Depending on your BIOS manufacturer and version, you can have up to five different settings. Let's look at these in the order of their importance.

Step 1   The most important setting, the *floppy drive controller* (FDC), can handle two floppy drives; it must be enabled for floppy drives to function in the PC. Enter the CMOS setup program by pressing the appropriate key or key combination (which you should remember from Lab Exercise 4.02) while your system is booting.

Having previously browsed through your version of CMOS, you should be able to locate the screen that contains settings for the FDC (often Integrated Peripherals, or I/O Device Configuration as in Figure 8-5). If you can't remember which screen deals with the FDC, browse through the CMOS screens until you find it.

Do you have an option in CMOS to disable the FDC? _____

Under what title heading did you find this option? _____

How do you disable this setting? _____

Do it! Disable it!

✔ Hint

Disabling the FDC is a good way for a network administrator to prevent users from either taking information off the network or introducing viruses into the network using floppies.

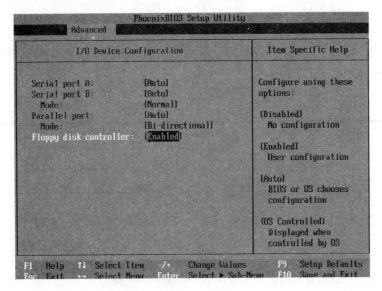

FIGURE 8-5 Locating the FDC settings

Step 2   Restart your system, and see if you can access the floppy drive. Did the LED on the front of the floppy drive turn on as the system booted up?

Step 3   Re-enter the CMOS setup utility, and turn the controller back on. Reboot the system, and test the floppy drive. Does it function properly?

Step 4   Re-enter the CMOS setup utility yet again—it's time to configure the second-most important setting for your floppy drive: the actual type of drive you have. Browse the CMOS setup utility, and locate the page that enables you to define the type of floppy drive you have.

✔ **Hint**

Because most every PC system has a floppy drive as a standard feature, try looking on the Standard (or Main) CMOS setup screen (see Figure 8-6).

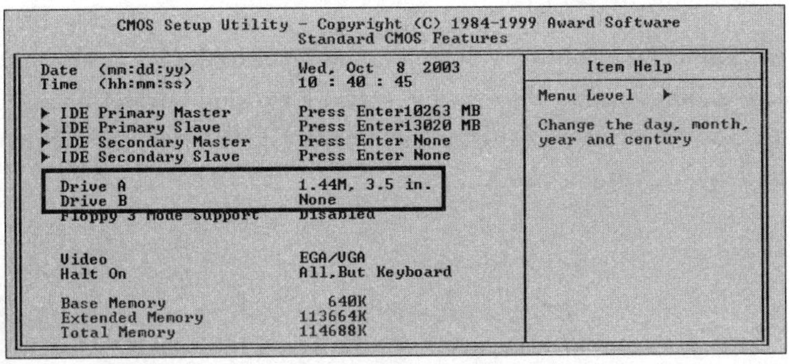

FIGURE 8-6 The Standard/Main CMOS setup screen

How many floppy drives can be supported on your system, according to CMOS? _____

How many floppy drives do you have set up on your system, according to CMOS? _____

How many different types of floppy drives can be set up on your system? _____

Do you have a None or Disabled setting? _____

How many different types of 5.25-inch drives can be set up? _____

How many different types of 3.5-inch drives can be set up? _____

What, if any, other types of drives can be set up? _____

Write down the Type setting of the floppy drive(s) on your system. _____

Now change the Type setting of floppy drive A: to None or Disabled. Don't worry; you'll set it back in a minute.

Step 5   Restart your system and see if you can access the floppy drive. Did the green LED on the front of the floppy drive turn on as the system booted up?

Step 6   Re-enter the CMOS setup utility and set your drive's Type back to its previous setting. Reboot the system again and test the floppy drive. Does it function properly?

Step 7   The next floppy drive setting to play with is the Boot Sequence (Figure 8-7). When you boot up a PC, the system must know where to get the operating system software to load into memory. The three standard places to store this software are the floppy drive, the hard drive, and the CD-ROM drive. Sometimes it's stored in another location, such as a network server.

Using the CMOS setup utility, you can designate the order in which your system will check the devices for the operating system software. Specifying the proper *boot sequence*—that is, the search order—saves time by telling the system where to look first. After all, why should your system waste time looking on the CD-ROM or floppy drive every time you boot, if your operating system is on the hard drive?

Enter the CMOS setup utility, and look for a screen that includes a Boot Sequence setting.

How many different boot sequences can you configure in CMOS? _____

How many different devices can be in the search sequence? _____

Set your system to boot from A: (the floppy drive) first.

Step 8   The other two floppy settings you need to know are Swap Floppy Drive and Boot Up Floppy Seek. Swap Floppy Drive, when enabled, enables you to change the logical location of drives A: and B: on the cable without removing the case and physically changing the drives. In other words, the drive on the end of the cable becomes the B: drive instead of the A: drive.

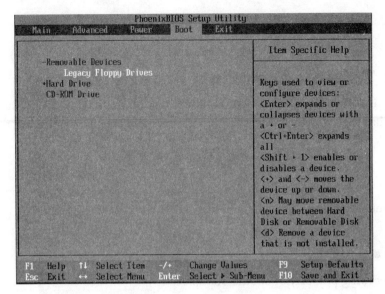

FIGURE 8-7 Floppy drive set in CMOS as first boot device

The Boot Up Floppy Seek setting controls checking the floppy drive when the system boots up. If enabled, BIOS will attempt to initialize the floppy drive. The drive activity light will come on, and you will hear the head moving back and forth in the drive. If the BIOS cannot detect a floppy drive, either because of improper configuration or because it is physically not there, it will flash an error message, but the system will still continue the boot process. Disabling this feature will skip the floppy drive check and speed up the boot process.

These two settings are not available in all CMOS setup utility programs, but are normally found with the BIOS features (see Figure 8-8).

Does your system have either or both of these settings? _____

Check all five of your floppy drive-related settings to be sure that they're correct.

Exit CMOS correctly, making sure to save any changes you might have made, if appropriate.

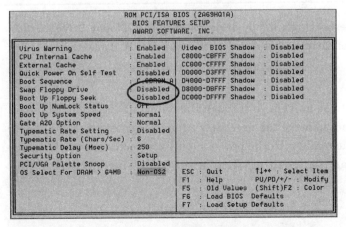

FIGURE 8-8 Finding the Swap Floppy Drive and Boot Up Floppy Seek settings

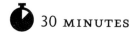 30 MINUTES

Lab Exercise 8.03: Troubleshooting Floppy Drives

An independent technician recently installed some devices in the PCs at your client's sales office. The client has called you, complaining that three floppy disk drives don't seem to work and begging you to come fix the systems.

Learning Objectives

In this lab, you'll use some basic troubleshooting skills that you learned in the first two lab exercises to test your floppy drive.

At the end of this lab, you'll be able to

- Determine if the drive is working properly or should be replaced

Lab Materials and Setup

The materials you need for this lab are

- A working computer system with a floppy drive installed

- A known good floppy disk

- Completion of Lab Exercises 8.01 and 8.02

Getting Down to Business

Before you get too far into this lab, note that floppy drives are inexpensive and should be replaced if found to be defective. A drive that costs $8 to $10 is much cheaper than paying a tech $50 per hour to try and repair it. That said, floppy disk drive problems most often lie in cabling, not in the drive itself. You can fix certain things quickly and efficiently, saving your clients time and money.

✔ **Cross-Reference**

To review the logical steps for troubleshooting a floppy drive, refer to the "Floppy Drive Maintenance and Troubleshooting" section of Chapter 8 of *Mike Meyers' A+ Guide to PC Hardware.*

Step 1 If you suspect your floppy drive to be broken, go through the following list and check each item. Any "no" answer means that you should make the necessary adjustments to the cables and/or BIOS settings. In extreme cases, the problem might be the power supply connector or even the power supply. My vote is always to look at the cables and settings first, before addressing the drive itself.

These questions are asked in the order of importance; to troubleshoot a floppy drive, you should check these items in order. Look at your PC, and answer these questions:

Is the floppy drive ribbon cable connected properly to both the motherboard and the floppy drive (floppy drive A: on the end of the cable nearest the twist, wire 1 to pin 1, connectors fully seated)? _____

Is the power connector connected fully and properly? Does it have the correct voltages needed (refer to the lab exercises in Chapter 7)? _____

Is the FDC enabled in BIOS? _____

Is the correct type of floppy drive indicated in BIOS? _____

Does the floppy drive LED come on for a short time and then turn off when you boot the system? _____

Step 2   If you've gotten this far, you know that the drive is installed and configured properly—but does it function correctly? Continue with the following questions. Any "no" answer means you should replace the drive:

Can you read a known good floppy disk? Remember, disks often go bad, so be sure to confirm that the disk works by testing it on another system. _____

Can you copy files to a known good floppy disk? _____

If you create a floppy disk on this drive, can you then read that disk in another floppy drive on a different system? _____

✔ **Hint**

One of the most annoying floppy drive problems is a disk stuck in the drive. This can happen when the metal portion of the disk becomes bent—you can get the disk into the drive with a little effort, but it catches on the edge of the case when you try to eject it. You can try sticking something non-conductive into the drive above or below the disk to help guide the disk past the frame; I've used a credit card for this task before! The safest way to do this, though, is to remove your PC case's faceplate (the front portion of the case that includes the floppy disk slot and usually the power button), and then eject the disk.

Lab Analysis Test

1. Kal cannot boot his system from his floppy drive with a known good bootable floppy disk. The cables are connected correctly, and the green LED lights up and then goes out during bootup, but he keeps getting the message "Disk Boot Failure." What is most likely the problem?

_____

_____

2. John was upgrading his system and decided to replace his cables because the old ones were fraying. He found some at a flea market that looked new at a very cheap price. Now his floppy does not work, and the LED stays lit continuously. What's going on?

_____

_____

3. Teresa has a 5.25-inch floppy disk that holds the only copy of the novel that she wrote many years ago. To recover this file, she needs to install an older 5.25-inch floppy drive. What will determine whether she can do this? Name at least two conditions.

_____

_____

4. Joe seems to have a problem with his floppy drive. When he changes the disk, the new disk is not recognized unless he reboots the system. What is the most likely cause of this condition?

_____

_____

5. You've been asked to install a new system without a floppy drive. What must you do in order to prevent floppy drive error messages during the boot process?

_____

_____

Key Term Quiz

Use the following vocabulary terms to complete the following sentences. Not all of the terms will be used.

3.5-inch floppy drive

5.25-inch floppy drive

A: drive

B: drive

boot sequence

FDC

LED

pin 1

pin 34

1. When you changing floppy disks, the system places a voltage signal on _____ to report the change.

2. The twist in the floppy ribbon cable determines which floppy drive is the _____.

3. A PC system can boot from multiple devices. The order in which it searches those devices is known as the _____.

4. You can easily tell by observing the _____ that you've plugged the floppy drive ribbon cable in backwards.

5. The most common type of floppy disk drive today is the _____.

Chapter 9

Hard Drive Technologies

Lab Exercises

As the primary storage area for the operating system, applications, and the ever-precious data, the hard drive takes on a level of importance to PC users that borders on reverence. Considering the fact that the death of a drive can mean many hours or days of tediously painful rebuilding, reloading applications, and re-creating data, such strong feelings make sense. And that reverence can turn quickly to agony if the user hasn't backed up his or her data in a while when the hard drive dies!

Every tech must know how to connect, configure, maintain, and troubleshoot hard drives of all sorts. A fully operational drive requires hardware knowledge, CMOS configuration, and software setup usually performed by tools that come with the operating system. The labs in this chapter cover physical installation and CMOS configuration of the mainstream hard drive technology, namely Integrated Drive Electronics (IDE), in both parallel and serial flavors. The other technology, Small Computer Systems Interface (SCSI), gets its very own Chapter 12 in the book.

 1 HOUR

Lab Exercise 9.01: Installing Parallel ATA Hard Drives

The local non-profit where you volunteer has received a donation of ten used PCs. Most of them have tiny hard drives and need an upgrade before you can distribute them to the various workers at the agency. All of the motherboards have built-in parallel ATA (PATA) controllers; some even have the better ATA/100 controllers. Your boss breaks out a stack of donated hard drives and tells you to get to work!

Installing a PATA hard drive successfully requires little more than connecting data and power cables to the drive and plugging the other end of the data cable into the motherboard. Sounds simple enough on the surface, but because all PATA drives give you options to install two on each motherboard controller, unwary techs get tripped up here. This lab walks you through the first major step in drive installation: the physical part.

✔ **Hint**

As you know from Chapter 9 of your textbook, IDE drives have several names that techs use pretty much interchangeably: IDE, EIDE, and ATA. You'll see all three terms in this lab manual and on the A+ Certification exams. Except for discussions of very old technology, the terms describe the same type of hard drive today.

Learning Objectives

In this lab exercise, you'll identify the different components of PATA hard drives and cables and learn installation procedures.

At the end of this lab, you'll be able to

- Remove a hard drive safely and correctly

- Describe PATA cables and connectors

- Describe the geometry of a hard drive

- Calculate the capacity of a hard drive

- Describe jumper settings

- Identify the major parts of a hard drive

- Install a hard drive safely and correctly

Lab Materials and Setup

The materials you need for this lab are

- A working PC with an ATA hard drive installed

- The Windows operating system on the PC

- Access to one or more broken hard drives that have the covers removed for observation of the internal parts (optional)

Getting Down to Business

Grab your handy screwdriver and anti-static wrist strap; it's time to remove a hard drive!

Step 1   Shut down your system, and remove the system cover, following proper electrostatic discharge (ESD) procedures.

Step 2   Disconnect all the ribbon cables from the hard drives and CD-ROM drives, but first note which device is connected to which cable and where the orientation stripe is located on each device. Be careful but firm. Grasp the cable as closely as possible to the connector on the drive and pull, rocking gently side to side.

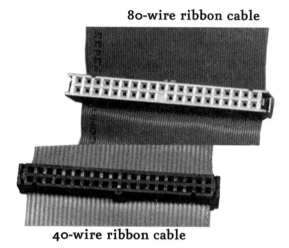

80-wire ribbon cable

40-wire ribbon cable

FIGURE 9-1 ATA cables: Comparing 80-wire and 40-wire ribbon cables

Examine the connector on the end of the ribbon cable. Use Figure 9-1 to help you.

How many holes does it have for pins? _____

Are any of the holes in the connector filled in? Does the connector have a raised portion on one side so that it only fits one way? In other words, is it *keyed*? _____

Take a close look at the top connector in Figure 9-1.

How many connectors are on your ribbon cable? _____

Do you have a 40-wire or 80-wire ribbon cable? _____

Disconnect the power supply from all of the PATA devices by unplugging the Molex connector from each one.

✖ Warning

Molex plugs can be difficult to remove and brutal on the fingers. There are little "bumps" on each side of the plug that will allow you to rock the plug back and forth to remove it.

Step 3   Now look at the motherboard connections, and note the orientation of how the cables are attached. Disconnect the ribbon cables from the motherboard. Be careful but firm. Grasp the cable as closely as possible to the connector on the motherboard and pull, rocking gently side to side.

Lay the cables aside for later reinstallation.

Step 4   Look at the ATA connections on your motherboard (see Figure 9-2).

ATA 66/33
controllers

Standard floppy
and
IDE controllers

FIGURE 9-2 Viewing the ATA connectors on a motherboard

Are the connectors on your motherboard freestanding? Or surrounded by plastic?

_____

Are they keyed (are there notches or missing pins to prevent you from plugging them in backward)?

_____

What color are they? _____

Look closely at your motherboard, and see if you can find writing on the board next to the IDE connections that indicates the proper pin orientation (pin 1).

Count the pins. How many are there? _____

Do you see any missing pins where a key in the connector might align? _____

Step 5   Remove a hard drive from the system and, being careful to note the type of screws you removed, store them for safekeeping. Be sure to use proper ESD procedures when removing the drive from your system.

Because of the variety of cases, caddies, bays, slots, and so on, it's not possible to give detailed instructions on how to remove the drive from your particular system. Look closely for caddy releases or retaining screws. Close inspection and a little logic will usually make it clear how to remove the drive. Make notes of how the drive comes out; you'll have to reinstall it later.

Step 6   With the hard drive out of the system and in a static-free place, ground yourself, pick it up, and examine it carefully.

Note its dimensions. It should measure about 6 × 3.5 × 1 inches. Some drives may be larger than this, measuring 6 × 5.25 × 1 inches—these are known as *bigfoot* drives. Some drives are smaller, but those are used mostly in laptops.

Look at the largest surfaces of the drive (the top and bottom). The bottom is where the printed circuit board with a read-only memory (ROM) chip is located. This circuitry is the hard drive controller. The top side of the drive normally has a label or other means of listing the specifications for the drive, but this may not always be the case.

Write down all the information on the label. Be sure to include the manufacturer and the model number for future reference.

_____

_____

Usually the label lists the three main measurements of hard drive geometry, the number of cylinders, the number of heads, and the number of sectors per track. Together they may be listed simply as CHS.

✔ Cross-Reference

For more information about CHS, refer to the "Geometry" section of Chapter 9 of *Mike Meyers' A+ Guide to PC Hardware.*

Using these three measurements, you can calculate the capacity of the hard drive. The formula is cylinders × heads × sectors per track × 512 = bytes of data. (The number of bytes in one sector is 512.)

For example, an older drive has the following information on the label. What is the total capacity of this drive?

- C = 859
- H = 16
- S = 63

859 × 16 × 63 × 512 = 443,326,464 bytes (that is millions of bytes)

To convert this to megabytes, divide the answer by 1,048,576.

443,326,464 /1,048,576 = 422.8 MB

A Seagate ST310211A PATA hard drive has CHS values of 16383, 16, and 63. What is its total capacity in bytes? In megabytes? In gigabytes? (To convert from megabytes to gigabytes, divide the number of megabytes by 1024.)

_____

_____

Step 7 Look at the end of the drive where the ribbon cable connects. Find the markings for where pin 1 of the ribbon cable should go.

Is it closer to the center of the drive near the power connector or to the side of the drive?

_____

Referring to Figure 9-3, does your hard drive have jumpers like these? _____

Notice the drive in Figure 9-3 has the jumper set to CS (which stands for "cable select").

Each PC system that boots from a PATA hard drive must have the hard drive located on the first PATA cable (IDE1), and it must have the jumper set to Master for it to be recognized as the boot drive. A second drive (hard drive or CD/DVD-media drive) can be on the same cable but must be set to Slave.

How are the jumpers set on your hard drive? _____

How are the jumpers set on your CD or DVD drive? _____

Can you have two master drives in the system? _____

For the purposes of this exercise, make sure you have your hard drive jumpered as it was *when you removed it.*

Step 8   Locate a broken hard drive (ask the instructor for one), and remove the cover.

✖ **Warning**

Never remove the cover from a functioning hard drive! Hard drives are extremely sensitive, and exposing the inside to the air will cause *irreparable* damage.

FIGURE 9-3 Locating the PATA hard drive jumper setting

Notice the round polished platters that spin in the middle of the drive. This is where the data is stored magnetically.

The arms that can move across the platters at an angle have tiny coils of wire attached to the ends of each arm and hold the read/write heads.

How many surfaces does your sample drive have (one platter = two surfaces)? _____

How many physical heads does your sample drive have? _____

Both answers are most likely the same because usually there is a read/write head for each surface.

Look at Figure 9-4, and identify the following parts by number.

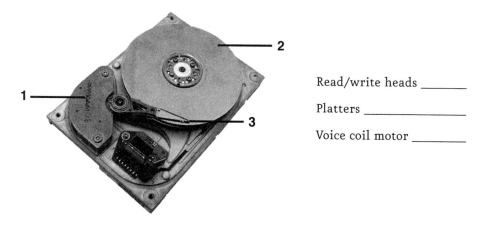

Read/write heads _____

Platters _____

Voice coil motor _____

FIGURE 9-4 The internal parts of a hard drive

Now look at Figure 9-5, and match the numbered components.

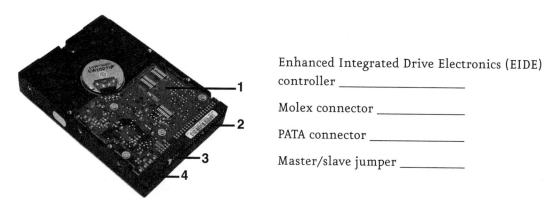

Enhanced Integrated Drive Electronics (EIDE) controller _____

Molex connector _____

PATA connector _____

Master/slave jumper _____

FIGURE 9-5 Viewing the external parts of a hard drive

Step 9 Insert the drive back into your system, and secure it with the proper screws. Connect all the ribbon cables to all the drives, and pay attention to the proper alignment of the connectors. Connect the Molex power connectors.

Leave the system case off until you verify everything works okay.

In order to verify, you need to go to the next major step in the process of hard drive installation, CMOS configuration. Lab Exercise 9.02 in this chapter covers the CMOS details, but if you just can't wait for the next lab to start, try this bonus step. It should work on modern motherboards.

Step 10 Turn on the system, and wait for it to boot to the Desktop. Select the My Computer icon, and double-click to open the window. Confirm that the hard drive(s) and CD-ROM icons are displayed. That you can even see your Desktop displayed confirms you have reinstalled the boot drive correctly, but do the other drives (if you have them) and your CD-ROM drive work?

✔ **Hint**

If you cannot boot the system or the CD-ROM drive does not work, the first and obvious place to start is to verify all the cable connections. Any kind of disk errors at this time were most likely caused by the technician. It worked before you touched it.

 30 MINUTES

Lab Exercise 9.02: Configuring CMOS Settings

The second major step in hard drive installation requires you to configure the BIOS for the hard drive properly. In the old days, you had to go into the CMOS setup utility and type in the geometry settings for a specific drive, but modern motherboards have autodetection capabilities that handle this function for you. Autodetection does not render CMOS irrelevant, though. You can do or undo all kinds of problems in CMOS relating to hard drives. This lab walks you through the important configuration options.

Learning Objectives

At the end of this lab, you'll be able to

- Configure the CMOS settings for the hard drive
- Confirm that the hard drive is indeed installed properly

Lab Materials and Setup

The materials you need for this lab are

- A fully functioning PC with a PATA hard drive

- A second drive with no important data (optional)

✔ **Hint**

It's actually a plus if your computer has the older Award BIOS because newer BIOS utilities give less control to the user.

Getting Down to Business

There are many possible CMOS settings for the hard drive, depending on the BIOS installed on the motherboard. For example, every motherboard gives you the option to disable the built-in hard drive controllers. Why is this relevant? You can install a drive into a perfectly good system and it won't work if the controllers are disabled!

Step 1 Turn on your system, and enter the CMOS setup utility by pressing the appropriate keystroke combinations while your system is booting.

Select the Integrated Peripherals option from the main menu, and look for the IDE controllers. You can enable or disable the controllers here.

✔ **Hint**

This option may look somewhat different depending on the version of CMOS you are using. Look for a menu option such as one of these:

- Onboard Primary PCI IDE

- Onboard Secondary PCI IDE

- PCI Primary and Secondary IDE

- Onboard IDE

When the controllers are disabled in CMOS, no device attached to them can be used—not even the CD-ROM or Zip drives. That is why some systems will not let you disable the primary and secondary IDE controllers at all.

If you jumped into this lab directly from Lab Exercise 9.01 and you've been on the edge of your seat because you don't know whether or not you installed and jumpered the drive correctly, here's where you find out.

Make sure both controllers are enabled and then look for the Autodetection option in the CMOS settings. Older systems have a separate category in CMOS, appropriately named Autodetect or something like that; newer systems have it integrated into the main settings screen. In either location, run the utility now. If your hard drive shows up in Autodetect as the drive you thought it would be—such as primary master, secondary master, and so on—then you installed and jumpered it properly.

Return to the main menu, and select the menu option for the screen containing the geometries for the system's hard drive(s). Depending on your version of CMOS, usually the geometries can be reached from the standard CMOS setup screen, as shown in Figure 9-6.

Look at the standard CMOS screen, and locate the hard drives. Again, depending on your BIOS they can be listed different ways, but the newer Award BIOS will list them as Primary Master, Primary Slave, Secondary Master, and Secondary Slave (see Figure 9-7).

Step 2   Save your settings, exit CMOS, and reboot your PC. You should boot into Windows normally. Check My Computer to verify you can see and access all drives.

Step 3   Reboot your PC and go into CMOS. Access the settings to enable or disable the IDE controllers and disable them both. (This won't affect your data, just drive access for the next couple of steps in this lab.)

Step 4   Save your settings, and exit CMOS to reboot the system. Making sure there is no floppy disk in the floppy drive, reboot normally and watch the monitor display for messages.

What message is displayed last?

_____

_____

With most systems, the PC will go through an entire process of looking for a bootable drive connected to an EIDE or SCSI controller, a CD-ROM drive, a network connection, and a floppy disk (not necessarily in that order) and then stop if it cannot find the operating system. It will then display a message and wait for you to insert a floppy disk to continue.

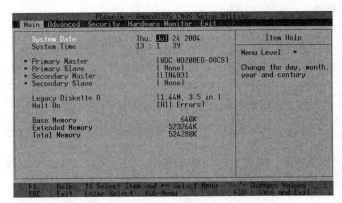

FIGURE 9-6 Hard drives listed as Primary Master, Primary Slave, Secondary Master, and Secondary Slave

✖ Warning

If your system is connected to a network and uses the network boot option, disconnect the network cable for this exercise to get the desired results. Be sure to plug the network cable back in when finished.

When the system is not able to find a disk (because you disabled the controller), it will probably hang for a long period of time and then return a Primary Hard Drive Failure code or error message. Some systems try to recognize that you have a hard drive regardless of the disabling of features, but this is rare.

Okay, so it can't find your hard drive. You obviously know why—you turned off the controller!

Step 5   Reboot your system, and enter the CMOS setup utility by pressing the appropriate keystroke combination while your system is booting. On the main menu, select the IDE HDD Auto Detection option (see Figure 9-7).

What happened when you selected IDE HDD Auto Detection this time and pressed ENTER to look for a drive? Why?

_____

_____

Step 6   The Auto Detection utility cannot see the hard drive because the controller is disabled. On the main menu screen, select Integrated Peripherals and enable the controllers. Now that the controllers are enabled, go back to the Auto Detection utility and look for any drives connected.

If Auto Detection still does not see a hard drive, save your settings, reboot your system and re-enter the CMOS setup utility. Then try it again.

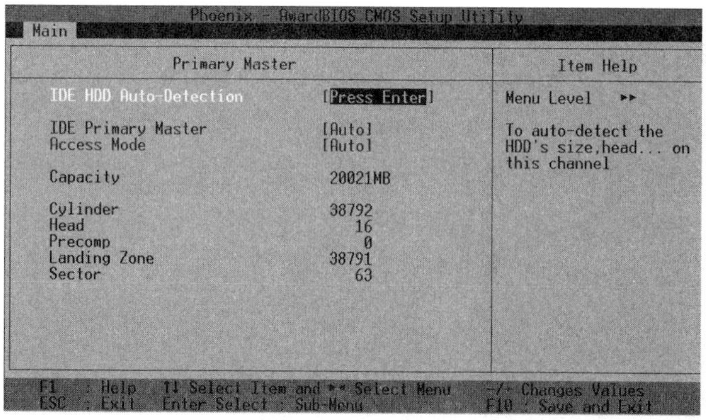

FIGURE 9-7 Selecting IDE HDD Auto Detection

Step 7 It is now time to show you the power of IDE HDD Auto Detection. Select it from the main menu, and watch what appears on the monitor screen. The system will find your primary master hard drive. Somewhere—and you may need to look closely to see this on some CMOS setup programs—you'll see two or three options for setting up your hard drive geometries. If you have a modern CMOS, you may not see this option or it may be preset and unchangeable. If this is the case for your CMOS, skip ahead to step 8!

Notice option 2(Y) on the top of the list. Also notice the flashing N on the screen. N is the default, and by pressing ENTER you would skip this drive altogether. *Do not* press ENTER unless you want to skip this drive. Under the Mode column, logical block addressing (LBA) means the BIOS supports all drive capacities of more than 504 MB. You must press 2 or Y to select this as the proper drive for your system.

Look along the bottom of the screen for this comment: Some OSs (like SCO UNIX) Must Use "Normal" for Installation. This is why there is a choice on this screen. Because you run Microsoft Windows software that supports LBA, select the top option by pressing 2 or Y followed by ENTER.

If you have more than one hard drive, step through each subsequent menu option, again selecting LBA.

Step 8 Now confirm the hard drive is listed properly in the standard CMOS setup. From the main menu, select the standard CMOS setup screen.

Is the primary master listed? _____

What is the Type setting? _____

What is the Size setting? _____

What is the Cylinder setting? _____

What is the Head setting? _____

What is the Mode setting? _____

Are there any other drives listed? _____

Exit CMOS correctly, making sure to save any changes you made.

Step 9 At this point if you did everything as described and if you started with a known good hard drive containing a working operating system, the system will now boot back into that operating system. Otherwise, if the instructor gave you a demo hard drive to use with nothing on it, then you'll have to wait until you partition and format the drive to see if all is okay.

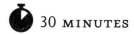 30 MINUTES

Lab Exercise 9.03: Installing Serial ATA Hard Drives

A wealthy donor has just given your non-profit company a brand new server machine, a dual-CPU hot rod with built-in serial ATA (SATA) controllers, but the SATA hard drives have yet to be installed or configured. You're tasked to do the job!

Installing SATA hard drives is a simple matter of plugging in the data and power cables to the drive and attaching the other end of the data cable to the SATA controller card or motherboard connection. You don't have to pull the power from the PC. You don't even have to shut down Windows. No, really. It's that simple! Let's go through the steps.

Learning Objectives

This lab touches on important tech skills, teaching you how to research hardware so you can provide good information to clients, and how to install what you've researched.

At the end of this lab, you'll be able to

- Explain key features of SATA

- Install a SATA hard drive

Lab Materials and Setup

The materials you need for this lab are

- Access to a PC system and the Internet

- Serial ATA controller and hard drive

Getting Down to Business

Limber up your surfing fingers as you'll do the Internet search for Eternal Truth first, but keep the screwdriver handy for the install that follows.

Step 1 Access the Internet, and search for the Promise SATA150TX2plus controller board.

Then answer these questions:

What is the speed of data transfer with ATA/133 drives? _____

What is the speed of data transfer with SATA/150 drives? _____

How many drives can be attached? _____

How large can the drives be? _____

Will it work with Windows 9x/Me? 2000? XP? _____

What is the cheapest price you can find? _____

Refer to your textbook, and answer these questions:

What is the maximum length of a SATA cable? _____

How many wires are in a SATA cable? _____

What is the maximum length of an 80-wire PATA cable? _____

How many drives can a single SATA cable support? _____

What is the eventual throughput speed of SATA? _____

SATA RAID has waltzed into the mainstream today. Motherboards are now being sold with a SATA RAID controller from Promise and other companies built in. Plus you can readily buy a PCI SATA RAID controller at your local computer parts store. They're becoming so common now, that soon you'll probably find them at Wal-Mart or Target!

✔ **Cross-Reference**

For more information on RAID, refer to the "Protecting Data with RAID" section of Chapter 9 of *Mike Meyers' A+ Guide to PC Hardware*.

Step 2 Access the Internet and go to this web site: http://www.promise.com. Select Fast Track S150 TX4, and then access the data sheet for specifications. If the site is not available, try searching http://www.google.com for the board by name: Fast Track S150 TX4.

✖ **Warning**

The system you're using must have Adobe Reader installed to view this data sheet. If it's not already installed, ask for permission from the instructor before downloading any programs, in case it is against school policy.

What is the greatest speed of data transfer? _____

How many serial ports/drives does it support? _____

What RAID configurations does it support? _____

Will it work with Windows 9x/Me? 2000? XP? _____

How large can the drives be? _____

Step 3 Write out two recommended hard drive setups, one for a customer who wants a very fast system and the other for a customer who cares very much about keeping his data secure. What hardware configurations did you choose? Why?

_____

_____

_____

_____

Step 4   It's time to get to work installing some SATA drives. With the PC powered down, remove the cover from the PC system unit that has the SATA controller installed and, after grounding yourself, pick up a SATA hard drive.

Step 5   Plug the SATA power connection into the drive; then connect the small SATA ribbon cable to the drive and to the controller. Now boot the PC.

> ✔ **Hint**
>
> If you haven't loaded drivers for the SATA controller, you should do so now. Otherwise, this is going to be a very frustrating lab for you!

Windows should pick up the drive with no problems at all. Check My Computer to verify the drive is installed and functional. (If the drive has no partition, it won't show up in My Computer, of course. If that's the case, use the Computer Management console—or FDISK in Windows 9x/Me—to verify that the drive works.)

Step 6   With Windows still running, disconnect the SATA data cable. What happened? _____

Step 7   Plug the data cable back in. Does Windows see the drive? _____

Step 8   Try the same hot-swap test with the SATA power cable (unplug then plug back in). Does this produce the same effect as the hot swap with the data cable? _____

 1 HOUR

Lab Exercise 9.04: Troubleshooting Hard Drive Installations

The newest tech in your office has had trouble installing hard drives properly. In fact, he's tried it on four different machines with eight different drives and only succeeded once! You've been tasked to troubleshoot his failed installations and patiently explain the proper installation process to him. What fun!

Learning Objectives

This lab walks you through the errors new techs typically make on hard drive installation, particularly with PATA drives.

At the end of this lab, you'll be able to

- Troubleshoot hard drive installation problems effectively

- Explain the proper installation techniques for PATA drives

Lab Materials and Setup

The materials you need for this lab are

- Access to a PC system

- At least one, but preferably two or more PATA hard drives

Getting Down to Business

It might seem odd to mess up a hard drive installation deliberately, but you can't hurt anything so give it a whirl. Seeing how the PC responds to mistakes when you know specifically what's wrong helps you in the field when you run into similar situations.

Step 1 You have to have a properly functioning PC for this lab to be effective, so verify first that you have a system up and running with one or more hard drives installed.

Step 2 Power down the system. Reverse the data cable for the hard drive on one end—that is, the controller or the drive, but not both—and then power up the system. What happens? Will the PC autodetect the drive? How should the ribbon cable be installed?

_____

Step 3 Power down the PC and put the cable back on properly.

Step 4 Change the jumper for the primary master hard drive to slave and power on the PC. What happens? Will the PC autodetect the drive? How should the jumper be installed?

_____

_____

Step 5 Power down the PC and put the jumper back on properly.

Step 6 Install a second drive onto the primary controller; set the jumpers on both drives incorrectly. Try variations: both as master; both as standalone; both as slave; both as cable select. Power on the PC and test each variation. What happens? Will the PC autodetect the drive? How should the jumpers be set for two PATA drives to work properly on the same controller?

_____

_____

Lab Analysis Test

1. Your friend brings a hard drive to you and asks if you can figure out how much data it can hold. On the label you find the numbers 12238C 16H 63S. What is the capacity of this drive in megabytes?

   _____

   _____

2. In what situation(s) might it be appropriate to disable the motherboard's hard drive controllers?

   _____

   _____

3. A new tech in your firm informs you that the PC he's working on can't autodetect a hard drive he installed. He thinks the motherboard is broken. What's the more likely problem here?

   _____

   _____

4. The second SATA hard drive on your company's server has just died. You have a replacement drive, but it's critical that the server stay up and function. What, if anything, can you do to resolve this problem and get the second drive replaced?

   _____

   _____

5. How could you jumper four PATA hard drives in a single system? Assume a standard motherboard with two IDE controllers.

   _____

   _____

Key Term Quiz

Use the following vocabulary terms to complete the following sentences. Not all of the terms will be used.

autodetect

cable select

CHS

master

PATA

platters

RAID

SATA

slave

1. The first drive on a cable is set to master. The second drive should be set to _____.

2. The data in a hard drive is actually stored magnetically on disks called _____.

3. One type of IDE drive transfers data in a parallel fashion. The other type of IDE drive transfers data in a serial fashion. The two types are _____ and _____, respectively.

4. To secure data in servers and high-end PCs, a _____ controller is used.

5. A great way to determine if you have a newly installed drive installed and configured correctly is to run _____.

Chapter 10

CD and DVD Media

Lab Exercises

The term "CD and DVD media" is an umbrella term for all devices that use those shiny discs that collect around your PC like pizza boxes in a fraternity house. You commonly hear those called CDs (for *compact discs*) or DVDs (for *digital versatile discs*). Both types of discs need a special drive to read or write the information recorded on the surface. Over the years, technology has developed single drives for CDs and DVDs, and today companies sell single drives that can both read and write CDs or DVDs. Some of the names of the drives include CD-ROM, CD-R (recordable), CD-RW (rewritable), DVD, and DVD+R/+RW.

The labs in this chapter teach you essential skills in installing and troubleshooting CD and DVD media drives. The principles follow those of PATA hard drive installation for the most part, so this should be a walk in the park for you!

30 MINUTES

Lab Exercise 10.01: Installing CD and DVD Media Drives

Your supervisor calls you in one day and announces that he wants to simplify the database backup procedures for your company. Specifically, he wants all the CD-R/RW drives on your company's servers replaced with the latest DVD-R/RW drives. The increased storage capacity of this type of drive will allow for a single disc to be used to back up an entire server system. To accomplish this task, you must physically uninstall all the existing CD-R/RW drives and replace them with DVD-R/RW equivalents.

You should be comfortable removing and installing CD and DVD media drives into and out of your PC. Fortunately, the vast majority of CD and DVD media drives use the popular PATA interface to connect to your system, making the installation process fairly simple.

Learning Objectives

In this lab, you'll remove and inspect a CD-ROM or DVD drive.

At the end of this lab, you'll be able to

- Understand how to remove and install CD-ROM or DVD drive safely and properly

- Know the physical features of a CD-ROM or DVD drive

Lab Materials and Setup

The materials you need for this lab are

- A working computer with Windows 98, Windows Me, Windows 2000, or Windows XP and a CD-ROM or DVD drive installed

Getting Down to Business

Removing a CD and DVD media drive is almost too easy. The only real secret here is to remember which cable you removed and how they were oriented to make sure you can put it back! Also, CD and DVD media drives use the standard master/slave jumpers—these also need to be inspected to make sure that the CD drive runs properly on the PATA connection!

Step 1 Properly shut down your system, and remove the cover from all sides of the PC case so you can access the screws on both sides of the CD-ROM drive. Using proper ESD procedures, remove the CD-ROM drive from your system:

a) Unplug the connections: first unplug the Molex plug from the back of the CD-ROM drive and then remove the PATA ribbon cable from the CD-ROM connector. Unplug the audio cable coming from the sound card (if present) that plugs into the back of the CD-ROM drive.

b) Using a Phillips head screwdriver, remove the screws holding the CD-ROM drive in place. Notice that the screws are small threaded screws—the same type you encountered when you removed and installed your floppy drive.

✔ **Hint**

Some CD-ROM drives are held in their bays by rails. Simply squeeze the rail toggles (sticking out the front), and remove the CD-ROM drive by pulling it forward.

Step 2 Inspect the CD-ROM drive. Look at the front of the drive where you insert a CD. See the tiny hole near the edge of the tray door? You can take a straightened-out paper clip and push it into this hole to release the CD tray. This is handy in case you accidentally leave a CD in the drive prior to removing it from the system. Go ahead and push a straightened-out paper clip into the hole to eject the tray.

Look at the back of the drive. You should see several areas for connections:

- The Molex power connection.

- The connection for the flat ribbon cable. This is usually a 40-pin EIDE connection.

- An audio connection for a cable to the sound card. There may be more than one connector because of different styles of cables, but only one cable should be connected.

- Jumper settings: master, slave, and cable select.

✔ **Hint**

Look for the orientation of pin 1. It is usually closest to the power connection. This also applies to the SCSI connection on some systems.

Step 3 Reinstall the CD-ROM or DVD drive back into your system. It can be a master drive or a slave drive depending on what other PATA devices are installed. Figure 10-1 shows a properly installed CD-ROM drive.

Now answer these questions:

Did you fasten the drive using the correct screws? _____

Is the master/slave jumper set correctly? _____

Is the PATA cable connected properly? _____

Is the Molex plug fully inserted? _____

Is the audio cable connected to the drive? _____

Step 4 Leave the cover(s) off the system and boot the PC to the Windows Desktop.

Step 5 Select My Computer, and notice if the CD-ROM icon is present. If so, all is well. If not, repeat steps 2 and 3. Remember, the most common problem when installing hardware is a loose connection. Replace the covers.

FIGURE 10-1 Viewing a properly installed CD media drive

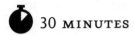 30 MINUTES

Lab Exercise 10.02: Troubleshooting CD and DVD Media

A coworker calls you and says that the CD-ROM drive on her computer won't read the CD that she put in the drive. She says that the drive is "making this horrible grinding sound" as the disc begins to spin. As an intrepid PC tech, you know that the issue she described could be caused by several things. You need to determine whether the CD-ROM drive in her computer is to blame, or if the CD media is damaged.

Malfunctioning CD media can be caused by either the discs or the drive itself. A technician's troubleshooting skills will help determine if the CDs are bad or the drive is malfunctioning. A malfunctioning drive can be caused by either a hardware or a software problem.

Learning Objectives

In this lab exercise, you'll examine symptoms and identify likely sources of CD media problems to help you increase your troubleshooting skills.

At the end of this lab, you'll be able to

- Identify CD or DVD problems

- Check the CD-ROM or DVD drive for hardware problems

- Verify software configuration settings

Lab Materials and Setup

The materials you need for this lab are

- A working PC system with Windows 98, Windows Me, Windows 2000, or Windows XP installed

- A CD-ROM or DVD drive

- Completion of Lab Exercise 10.01

Getting Down to Business

Get that cover off of your PC! Parts of this lab will require you getting into your system for answers!

Step 1 Identifying CD and DVD problems is a matter of observing and testing. Refer to the information in Lab Exercise 10.01, and answer the following questions:

You look at a CD and see a couple of small labels on it. It reads the data fine in a 10X-speed drive. Will this CD read okay in the higher 52X-speed drives? Why or why not?

_____

_____

List at least four environmental conditions that are bad for CDs.

_____

_____

_____

_____

Can you test CDs like floppy disks where you try the media in a different system before blaming the drive? Why or why not?

_____

_____

Step 2   You just installed a CD-ROM drive, and it is not showing up in the boot messages. The first place to check is the cabling; however, you should also check the BIOS settings.

Access the CMOS setup utility, and go to the standard CMOS setup screen. Depending on your BIOS manufacturer, the Type column should be set to CD-ROM or Auto.

What is yours set to? _____

Step 3   Your CD-ROM drive seems sluggish when transferring large amounts of data.

Access the Integrated Peripherals screen in your CMOS setup and see if the PIO/DMA settings are set properly for this drive.

What are your PIO/DMA settings? _____

✔ Hint

Auto settings will work fine for most newer motherboards. Some older motherboards allowed you to tweak the settings for drives that were newer than the BIOS. In these cases, you should use the fastest modes your drive will support.

Step 4   Okay, the BIOS is set correctly and your CD-ROM shows up in the My Computer window, but it still seems sluggish.

From the Windows 98 Desktop, select Start | Settings | Control Panel | System | Device Manager. Expand the CD-ROM heading, and highlight your CD-ROM drive. Now click the Properties button and then the Settings tab. Notice the choice for DMA. If your drive supports DMA, turn the DMA setting on.

How is your DMA choice set? On or off? _____

Or, do the following:

From the Windows 2000 or XP Desktop, navigate to the Device Manager. Expand the IDE ATA/ATAPI Controllers heading and highlight the Primary or Secondary IDE Channel option (depending where your CD-ROM drive is located). Now select the Properties icon at the top of the screen button and then the Advanced Settings tab. Notice the choice for Device 0 and Device 1 DMA. If your CD-ROM drive supports DMA, turn this choice on.

How is your DMA choice set? On or off? _____

✔ Hint

To determine if your device supports DMA, look up the device specifications on the Internet. Also, it might be printed on the box the device came in. Hard drives used to be the only things that were DMA capable, but now CD-ROM drives are also being sold as such. None of the Microsoft Windows operating systems come with DMA enabled by default, even if your hardware supports it. Therefore, you need to turn it on for any DMA-capable devices on your IDE channels to get the most out of them.

Lab Analysis Test

1. Joe installed a CD-ROM drive on the same cable as his primary hard drive, and now the system will not boot. What could be causing this?

   _____

   _____

2. While looking around in the BIOS settings, Teresa set the PIO and DMA settings to Auto. Will this affect the system in any way? Explain.

   _____

   _____

3. John has many audio CDs that he listens to with his PC CD-ROM drive while he is working. Sometimes the CD-ROM drive starts making a loud humming noise but stops when he removes the CD. What should John do?

   _____

   _____

4. When Bob puts his CD-RW in the drive and copies files to and from it, he notices that the drive speeds up and slows down. Is this normal? What should he do to fix it?

    _____

    _____

5. After removing a CD-ROM drive for replacement, you remember that you left a CD in the drive. You look for a hole to insert the paper clip into, but there is none. How do you remove the CD?

    _____

    _____

Key Term Quiz

Use the following vocabulary terms to complete the following sentences. Not all of the terms will be used.

CD-ROM drive

CMOS

disc

DMA

DVD

label

scratches

spiral

surface

1. A CD-ROM or DVD drive must be identified in the _____ settings.

2. The recording of data on a CD is done in a _____ fashion.

3. If the DVD supports _____, it must be enabled in Device Manager.

4. The top surface of the CD is where you can write or put a _____.

5. The reflective aluminum layer can be destroyed by _____.

Chapter 11

Video

Lab Exercises

Few components impact the PC user like the video system, the primary output for the PC. As you know from the textbook, the video system has two main hardware components—monitor and display adapter—that work together to produce the image on your screen. Both components must be installed and configured properly in Windows, otherwise your viewing pleasure becomes seriously compromised. Good techs know how to do video right!

In this set of labs, you'll install a display adapter, hook up a monitor, load video drivers, and configure Windows for optimal viewing. You'll also run though some typical troubleshooting issues most techs face when dealing with video.

 30 MINUTES

Lab Exercise 11.01: Installing Video

Your office staffs' computers need a serious video upgrade. Some of the PCs have tiny 14-inch CRT monitors that simply *have* to go. Others have decent 17-inch and 19-inch CRTs that have a year or two life in them. Your boss has bought new AGP and PCI video cards and some LCD monitors to replace the older CRTs. You're tasked with installing the cards, loading drivers, and setting everything up in Windows.

✖ Warning

It is critical to understand that only *trained* monitor technicians should remove the cover of a video monitor (or television). The inside of a traditional monitor might look similar to the interior of a PC, with printed circuit boards and related components, but there's a big difference: No PC has voltages up to +50,000 volts or more inside, and most CRT monitors do. So be sure to get one thing clear—casually opening a monitor and snooping around has the potential to become harmful to you and the monitor—and in cases of extreme carelessness, it's even deadly! Even when the power is disconnected, certain components (capacitors) still retain substantial levels of voltage for an extended period of time. Capacitors work like batteries. Yes, they can maintain 50,000 volts! If you inadvertently short one of the capacitors, a large discharge will occur into the monitor circuits, destroying them. If you're touching the metal frame, you could fry yourself—to death. Given this risk, certain aspects of monitor repair fall outside the necessary skill set for a standard PC support person and definitely outside the A+ test domains. Make sure you understand the problems you can fix safely and the ones you need to hand over to a monitor shop.

✔ **Cross-Reference**

For the details of CRT versus LCD monitors, refer to the "CRT and LCD Displays" section in Chapter 11 of *Mike Meyers' A+ Guide to PC Hardware*.

Learning Objectives

At the end of this lab, you'll be able to

- Identify the make and model of a video card

- Install a video display adapter card

- Check BIOS for proper video settings

- Adjust the monitor for the proper display

- Optimize the video settings in Windows

Lab Materials and Setup

The materials you need for this lab are

- A working PC with Windows 98, Windows Me, Windows 2000, or Windows XP installed

- A working monitor

✔ **Hint**

Classrooms that have a variety of different monitor types and video display adapter cards are a plus.

Getting Down to Business

To begin this lab, you'll become familiar with the video components in your system. You'll then step through the proper installation and configuration of a video adapter.

✖ **Warning**

Some versions of Microsoft Windows operating systems have problems when you make changes to the video display adapters, even when you're simply removing and reinstalling the same card into a different slot. If you perform this lab on a test machine, you should have no real problem if things go wrong. If you're using your primary PC to do the lab, however, make certain you have current drivers available for your video card or a source to get drivers if necessary.

Step 1 Shut down your system properly, and remove the cover from the PC to expose the expansion buses.

a) Find your video display adapter card (the one the monitor is attached to). What type of video display adapter is installed: ISA, PCI, or AGP? _____

b) Detach the monitor's cable from the video card.

Using good ESD avoidance procedures, remove the restraining screw and put it in a safe place, and then remove your video display adapter card. Examine it closely to answer the following questions (see Figure 11-1). Be careful not to touch the expansion slot contacts on the card.

c) Look for a name or model number on the board or chipset.

Who is the manufacturer, or what is the model number? Write it down. (Note that if you follow the scenario for this lab, you'd look up the information for the *new* video cards, not the old ones that you're about to donate to charity!)

_____

_____

Be sure to write down as much information as you can collect from the board and chips for a later assignment.

d) Reinsert the video display adapter into the same slot, and make sure it is properly seated. Reattach the monitor cable, and make sure you test your system with the case still open to see if it works. It can be frustrating and embarrassing to close the case, fire up the system, and get a video error. (Not that I've ever done that!)

✔ **Hint**

AGP cards can be a little tricky; they must be seated perfectly or they will not work.

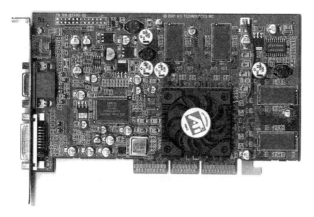

FIGURE 11-1 A video card with a cooling fan and four onboard RAM chips

e) Boot your system, and use a browser to search the Internet.

Search the Internet with the previous information you gathered about the manufacturer and model number.

Can you find the specifications for your video adapter? _____

What is the highest resolution you can achieve with your video adapter based on the specifications? _____

Are there any jumpers or switches on your video adapter? _____

How should they be set? _____

Is there a socket or sockets to add or upgrade the video RAM? _____

What other features make your video adapter unique?

_____

_____

Step 2 Reboot your system, and press the proper key sequence to enter the CMOS setup utility. Depending on the BIOS manufacturer and version, there can be as many as five or more video-related settings. My lab system has ten settings directly related to video or the AGP slot. Complete each of these questions based on your specific BIOS. Some of the names of the sections will undoubtedly differ from the ones presented below. Search around a bit and you'll find video options in your CMOS.

On the Standard CMOS Setup screen, how many choices are there for video, and how is your video set? _____

On the Chipset Features Setup screen, what is the value for your Video RAM Cacheable setting?

_____

On the Power Management Setup screen, do you have settings to control how the monitor and video adapter will react when not in use for a period of time? What are your settings? _____

_____

On the Integrated Peripherals screen, do you have an Init Display First setting? What are the choices? _____ and _____. What does your setting say? _____
Know that when this setting is wrong, the monitor display might not work.

Step 3 You'll now examine a monitor and see what sort of external controls it has. If you're not in a computer lab, go to your local computer store and examine a wide variety of monitors.

Figures 11-2 and 11-3 show the control buttons for adjusting the display attributes for an LCD and a CRT monitor, respectively. Both of these have the controls on the front of the monitor, but some have the controls behind a door under the front of the monitor, and others may have them on the back.

Figure 11-2 A multimedia LCD monitor with front-panel buttons for adjustments

Figure 11-3 A CRT monitor with a built-in function knob and an onscreen menu for adjustments

A monitor can have quite a few adjustable features. How many of the following can you adjust on your LCD monitor?

Brightness _____

Contrast _____

Clock _____

H-position _____

V-position _____

Color temperature _____

Auto balance _____

Sharpness _____

Gamma _____

Signal select (for LCDs with both VGA and DVI inputs) _____

Full screen _____

Language _____

How many of these can you adjust on your CRT monitor?

Brightness _____

Contrast _____

Color saturation _____

Vertical size   _____

Vertical position   _____

Horizontal size   _____

Horizontal position   _____

Pincushioning (for adjusting displays that are narrow in the middle
but flare out at the top and bottom)   _____

Keystoning (for adjusting displays that are narrow at the top but
flare out at the bottom)   _____

Degauss (for adjusting displays that have become fuzzy due to
electromagnetic interference)   _____

Play with the controls of your monitor or a test monitor. If the current settings use percentages, write down the settings before doing any adjustments. Then follow these steps:

a) Change the settings such as color and sizing. Really mess it up!

b) Put them back as close as possible to their original positions.

c) Optimize the screen for clarity and position.

Step 4 The hardware is set up properly and the BIOS settings should be correct, so now you need to configure and optimize the Windows settings that determine your video display characteristics. To do this, you need to get to the Display applet.

✔ Hint

This lab simulates a working PC that you upgrade with new hardware and drivers. All the steps can work just as well for installing a video card into a new system, although the pace of that installation would differ. In a new system, you install the video card but do not install the drivers at first. Second, you let Windows use generic VGA drivers until you make sure you can boot properly. Third, you would install the drivers for the video card. Finally, you'd go to the Display applet and optimize the video card settings.

✖ Warning

You're going to make changes to the look and feel of Windows. Making some of these changes can result in frustrating and time-consuming problems. Use a test machine if you have one available. If you must use your own machine, write down all your display settings before you make any changes.

There are several ways to navigate to the Display applet. You can follow these steps:

a)   Alternate-click your Windows Desktop.

b)   Select Properties from the drop-down menu.

c)   Select the Settings tab.

Or you can follow these steps:

a)   Go to the Control Panel.

b)   Double-click the Display applet icon.

c)   Select the Settings tab.

Choose one of these methods to get to the Display Properties dialog box's Settings tab. This tab displays the monitor settings, such as those shown in Figure 11-4:

- Resolution

- Number of colors

Each video display adapter manufacturer has different options for its cards. By clicking the Advanced button, you can access more information about the display adapter. You may see a choice for setting the refresh rate, as well as other features. Look through the settings on the Advanced tab, and see what your display adapter manufacturer provides. Remember that the video adapter "pushes" the monitor. If you set the refresh too high, it can destroy the monitor.

Write down your display's current resolution, color depth, and refresh rate.

_____

_____

Close the Advanced dialog box (if you selected it), but leave the Display Properties dialog box open.

Make some changes to the background and colors on your screen. You'll find these options on the Background and Appearance tabs, respectively. Be sure to note the original settings so you can change things back when you are done.

Change the Desktop background to something you might like better, such as Autumn or Bliss. Then follow these steps:

a)   Experiment with color combinations.

✔ Hint

This is perfectly safe and easy to undo.

FIGURE 11-4 The Display Properties dialog box's Settings tab

b)   Make some changes to the displayed fonts and menu bars.

c)   Add a screensaver, or change the one you currently have. You'll find these options on the Screen Saver tab. Play with the settings.

Experiment with changing the colors and resolution of your display.

Can your machine run in 16-bit color?   _____

How about 24-bit color?   _____

Can you run 800×600 resolution?   _____

Can you run 1024×768 resolution?   _____

Can you run 1280×960 resolution?   _____

Do you have any other options?   _____

Click the Advanced button again, and experiment with changing the refresh rate (see Figure 11-5).

✔ **Hint**

Because LCD monitors work the way they do, the refresh rate is not really applicable to them. As a general rule, LCD monitors display a stable, flicker-free image at 60 hertz (Hz). There are no visible differences between 85 Hz and 60 Hz.

Can you make specific numeric changes? _____

Are the Optimal and Adapter Default settings the only choices you have? _____

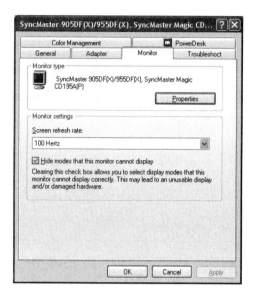

Figure 11-5 Viewing a typical refresh setting under the Monitor tab

---

✔ **Hint**

The refresh rate is not an option on all video adapters. This may be in a different location or not on your system at all.

Make sure you return all the settings to their original values, and close the Display Properties dialog box.

Check the drivers for your video card and monitor. Are they "standard" drivers, or are they specific to your hardware? Follow these steps:

a) Go to the Device Manager, locate your display adapter, alternate-click, and select Properties.

b) Locate your driver information.

c) Can you identify the version number(s) of your video drivers? Write them down.

_____

_____

d) Go online, and surf to the manufacturer's web site.

e) Check to see if there are any new drivers available.

f)   If new drivers are available, download and install them. (Do this on a test machine first. Get comfortable with the whole process before you do this on your personal computer.)

How did this affect your machine?

_____

_____

✔ **Hint**

New drivers will sometimes fail to work properly, thereby crippling your PC. Windows XP has the Driver Rollback feature that enables you to go back to a driver that worked correctly in case this happens.

Step 5   One more place to look for video settings is the Power Management Control Panel. Take a look at any power management settings you may have.

Go to the Control Panel, and double-click the Power Management or Power Options applet, if you have one.

Use the drop-down menu arrow to see what power management schemes are available.

Which one do you have running? _____

How long is the period of inactivity before your monitor shuts off? _____

Close the Control Panel.

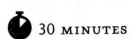

30 MINUTES

Lab Exercise 11.02: Troubleshooting Video

Video troubleshooting really boils down to two distinct questions. First, are the physical video components installed and configured properly (see Lab Exercise 11.01)? Second, do the current video display adapter and CPU support the software technologies they're trying to use? Or, have you loaded that killer game and completely overwhelmed your video subsystem?! In this lab exercise, you'll create connectivity problems to simulate real-world installation problems, and use the DirectX Diagnostic tool to analyze your system.

Learning Objectives

At the end of this lab, you'll be able to

- Recognize and fix typical installation and connectivity problems

- Use the Microsoft DirectX Diagnostic tool to analyze and test the graphic display attributes of a PC system

Lab Materials and Setup

The materials you need for this lab are

- A working PC with Windows 98 or newer installed (this lab will not work with Windows 95)

- Any version of the Microsoft DirectX Diagnostic tool installed

Getting Down to Business

If you went through Lab Exercise 11.01 and had typical results—video card not seated properly, forgetting to plug things in all the way, and so on—you can probably skip steps 1 and 2 of this lab. If you had a perfect reinstall, on the other hand, then definitely do steps 1 and 2 of this lab!

Step 1 Loosen the restraining screws holding the monitor data cable securely to the video card. With the system fully powered up and in Windows, gently disconnect the monitor cable partly.

What happened to the screen? _____

With many monitors, a loose cable results in a seriously degraded display. Colors fade out or a single color disappears; the display appears grainy or snow covered, and so on. If you run into such effects in the field, you know to check your connectivity!

Connect the monitor cable and tighten the restraining screws to resume normal operation.

Step 2 With the power off and disconnected from the PC, open the case and remove the restraining screw securing the video card to the case frame. Pull the video card up slightly on one end. Reapply electricity and power up the PC.

What happened? _____

You might have to run through this a couple of times to get the desired effect, which is a seemingly dead PC and some beeping from the system speaker. That long-short-short beep code, as mentioned in Lab Exercise 11.01, is pretty universally recognizable as the PC crying out loudly, "My video card is not seated properly. Help!"

With the power off and disconnected, reseat your video card, apply the restraining screw, and power up your PC to resume normal operation.

Step 3 Access the Microsoft DirectX Diagnostic tool using these steps:

a) Select Start | Programs | Accessories | System Tools | System Information.

b) Open the Tools menu.

c) Select DirectX Diagnostic tool (see Figure 11-6).

✔ **Hint**

Many technicians love the command line because it can save a lot of time. If you're one of them, try this: select Start | Run, and then type **dxdiag**. Click OK.

Step 4 Select the Display tab (see Figure 11-7).

What is the name of your display adapter? _____

How much total memory is on the adapter? _____

What is the current display mode? _____

What is the drive name and version? _____

Does it display a driver version date? _____

Should you look for a more current driver? _____

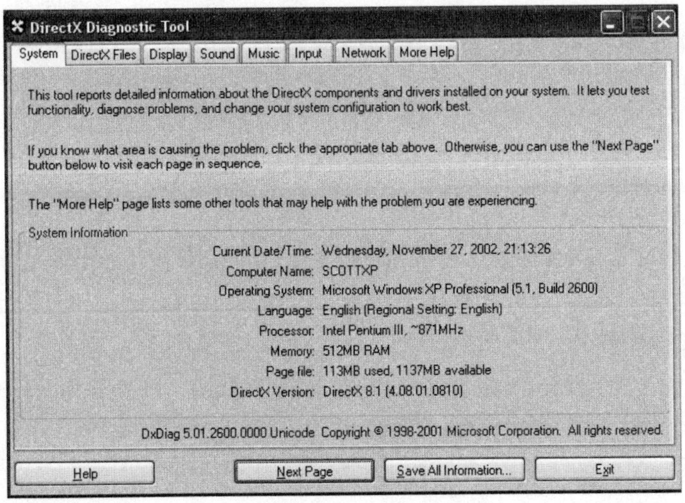

FIGURE 11-6 Using the DirectX Diagnostic tool

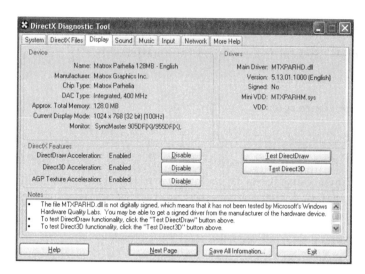

Figure 11-7 Viewing the DirectX Diagnostic tool's Display tab

Step 5   Look in the Notes box at the bottom of the Display tab, and read the information provided. This will show information for conflicts or problem areas.

Do you show any conflicting information? What does it report?

_____

_____

Step 6   Select and test the DirectDraw feature, and follow the instructions.

Did the test complete correctly? _____

Step 7   Select and test the Direct3D feature, and follow the instructions.

Did the test complete correctly? _____

Step 8   Some programs run very slowly or not at all unless Microsoft DirectDraw or Direct3D hardware acceleration is available. On the Display tab, look in the DirectX Features section to see whether Direct-Draw, Direct3D, or AGP texture acceleration is set to Not Available.

You may need to enable them or adjust your graphics acceleration, as described in the following steps. You might also consider upgrading your hardware if necessary to improve performance.

a)   Go to the Control Panel.

b)   Open Display, and select the Settings tab.

c)   Click Advanced, and select the Performance or Troubleshooting tab.

d)   Move the Hardware Acceleration slider to Full.

✔ **Hint**

If you're looking at a Windows XP system, the tab under the Advanced options for hardware acceleration is Troubleshoot.

Lab Analysis Test

1. If you remove an AGP video display adapter and replace it with a PCI video display adapter, what must you do to be sure the Windows Desktop will display properly?

   _____

   _____

2. Your nephew Johnny visited last night, and this morning your monitor is dead. What should you do first, second, and third?

   _____

   _____

3. What can happen if the refresh rate for a CRT is set too high?

   _____

   _____

4. Teresa installed a new game, but she is frustrated because it responds too slowly. What might she check?

   _____

   _____

5. Kal installed a new video display adapter, but the best setting he can adjust it to is 800 × 600 resolution with 256 colors. What must he do to make it go higher?

   _____

   _____

Key Term Quiz

Use the following vocabulary terms to complete the following sentences. Not all of the terms will be used.

color depth

DirectX Diagnostic

Display applet

hardware acceleration

Init display first

refresh rate

resolution

1. Once software is installed, test your video using Microsoft's _____ tool.

2. Erin's monitor was set to 640 × 480, a very low _____.

3. John complained constantly about getting headaches every day. When you looked at his PC, you noted that the screen flickered. John's monitor had the _____ set too low!

4. The _____ is the one-stop shop in Windows for changing your video settings.

5. _____ can offer excellent visuals in games and not bog down the system.

Chapter 12
SCSI

Lab Exercises

Small Computer System Interface (SCSI) is still king of the hard drives in servers but is beginning to lose ground in single-user systems. The inclusion of USB and Serial ATA (SATA) controllers on new motherboards leaves SCSI as an option mainly for super users. SCSI hard drives are generally faster—10,000 rpm—and more reliable. Furthermore, unlike EIDE, which is limited to two drives per controller, a single parallel SCSI host adapter can handle up to 15 devices (16 counting itself). The Ultra320 SCSI offers a blazingly fast transfer rate of 320 MBps; SATA is currently limited to 150 MBps.

SCSI can be best described as a "miniature network" inside your PC. Any type of peripheral can be built as a SCSI device. The most common SCSI devices, though, include hard drives, tape backup units, removable hard drives, scanners, CD-ROM drives, and printers. SCSI manifests itself through a SCSI *chain*, which is a series of SCSI devices working together through a host adapter.

In these lab exercises, you'll install a SCSI host adapter and some devices. The key for you in this chapter is to get as many different types of SCSI devices as you can find and put them together in a variety of ways.

 1 HOUR

Lab Exercise 12.01: Installing SCSI

The non-profit corporation where you work has just received a stack of SCSI host adapters and devices, none of which came with much documentation. You've been tasked to install the host adapters and connect the devices in a controlled lab, and then install the most useful ones in various staff members' PCs.

Learning Objectives

In this lab exercise, you'll install and configure SCSI devices.

At the end of this lab, you'll be able to

- Install a SCSI host adapter

- Install a SCSI hard drive

- Install an external SCSI device

- Create a SCSI chain

- Use the SCSI configuration utility

✔ Cross-Reference

For the scoop on everything SCSI, refer to Chapter 12 of the *Mike Meyers' A+ Guide to PC Hardware*.

Lab Materials and Setup

The materials you need for this lab are

- A working PC with Windows 98, Windows Me, Windows 2000, or Windows XP installed

- SCSI cables and terminators

- Both internal and external SCSI devices (the following items are recommended devices for a successful lab experience)

→ Note

You may not have access to the full range of SCSI devices required by this lab. In that case, read through the exercises, paying close attention to the images, and follow along as closely as you can with the included steps. If you have an external device and an internal device, then do steps 1, 2, 3, and 5 (substituting the device you have on hand for the hard drive in step 3) and read the rest.

- PCI Plug and Play (PnP) Adaptec 2940 (8-bit, narrow, SCSI-2) host adapter with both an internal and an external port. A comparable host adapter is okay as long as it has a way to enter and configure the ROM BIOS.

- Two SCSI hard drives, one with built-in termination

- External SCSI Zip drive or comparable

- Internal SCSI CD-ROM drive that requires resistor packs installed for termination

- Any other SCSI devices that may be available, including other hard drives and removable media drives

- Long SCSI 50-pin ribbon cable with four or more connectors

- Active or passive 50-pin terminating resistor

Getting Down to Business

SCSI host adapters require free resources—such as Interrupt Requests (IRQs), Input/Output (I/O) addresses, Direct Memory Access (DMA) channel, and memory addresses—and proper drivers. If you stick with a solid, well-known brand such as the Adaptec PnP models, you'll not have any problems with this lab.

With the exception of single-purpose host adapters, most every SCSI card has an onboard ROM chip that enables you to configure both the host adapter settings and the specific settings for the devices you'll plug into the adapter.

Step 1 The first task you need to do in any SCSI installation is to install the host adapter. Some motherboards may have it already built-in, so you would not need to install a separate adapter board. This exercise assumes you're installing a PCI SCSI host adapter.

Follow these steps to get started:

a) Shut your system down properly, and remove the PC cover. Unplug the power cord.

b) Using proper ESD procedures, insert the PCI SCSI host adapter into an open slot.

c) Do not connect any devices at this time.

d) Leave the system cover off, and reboot your system.

> **✷ Warning**
>
> Pay close attention early during the boot process or you will miss SCSI messages.

Step 2 Access the SCSI configuration utility so you can set up the host adapter properly. Here's how.

Notice the SCSI ROM messages during the boot process. Adaptec host adapters will flash or display the message "Press <Ctrl><A> for SCSISelect<TM> Utility!" (see Figure 12-1). You should see something similar when you boot your system. Follow the directions to enter the SCSI configuration utility. If you miss the SCSI message the first time, simply press CTRL-ALT-DELETE and watch again for the message.

> **✔ Hint**
>
> Not all SCSI host adapters give you access to the ROM BIOS. If you're not sure whether your host adapter does, look up the specifications of the board on the Internet.

```
    ⚠    American    Released:  08/21/2000
         Megatrends  AMBIOS (C) 1999 American Megatrends Inc.,
    7iXE4    F7

    Check System Health: OK
    Main Processor:  AMD-Athlon(tm)  650 MHz
    Checking NVRAM..

    WAIT...
    Pri Master:  IXACA54A IBM-DTLA-307075
                 Ultra DMA Mode-4, S.M.A.R.T. Capable and Status OK
    Sec Master:  1.00    PLEXTOR CD-R PX-W1610A

    Adaptec AHA-2940 Ultra/Ultra W BIOS v1.25
    (c) 1996 Adaptec, Inc. All Rights Reserved.

    ◀◀◀ Press <Ctrl><A> for SCSISelect(TM) Utility! ▶▶▶
```

Figure 12-1 Getting the Adaptec host adapter prompt for configuration

When you enter the configuration utility, you have several options. Figure 12-2 displays the options for the Adaptec 2940: Configure/View Host Adapter Settings and SCSI Disk Utilities.

✔ **Hint**

The following steps are based on the host adapter and devices pictured. If you are using different equipment, the steps may vary slightly, but use these steps to guide you through configuring your specific equipment.

Follow these steps:

a)   Select Configure/View Host Adapter Settings.

b)   Press F6 to reset to host adapter defaults. Because you are unaware of the previous use or settings of this adapter (at least as far as this scenario is concerned), it's best to start from the default settings.

c)   Check the termination setting, and be sure it's set to Automatic (see Figure 12-3).

d)   Check the Adapter SCSI ID, and be sure it's set to 7 (see Figure 12-3).

e)   Save the configuration and reboot. This time, allow your system to boot normally, and load any drivers Windows needs.

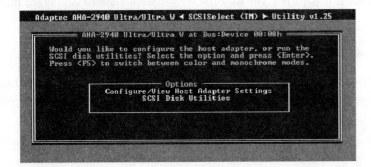

Figure 12-2 Viewing configuration options

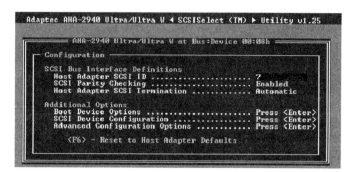

FIGURE 12-3 Setting the SCSI host adapter ID and termination

Check the host adapter in the Device Manager. Is the SCSI host adapter there? Are there any conflicts to be resolved? If so, resolve them, and then continue with the next step.

Step 3 Now you'll add SCSI devices. When installing a SCSI device, you need proper connectivity, including cabling and power; for some devices, you may also need to install Windows drivers. Most SCSI hard drives set up with no need for additional drivers. Let's begin by installing a SCSI hard drive.

✔ **Hint**

Each type of SCSI device including the host adapter has its own driver. Most likely the operating system installed a driver for the host adapter that assumes there is a hard drive attached. If you have Zip drives, CD-ROM drives, scanners or printers, they will need their own drivers. If you don't have them, use the Internet to download the correct ones.

Follow these steps:

a) Properly shut down your system.

b) Attach the SCSI hard drive to one of the connectors on the SCSI cable.

c) Check for jumpers and terminating resistors on the hard drive (see Figure 12-4).

d) Set your hard drive to ID 0.

e) Check the termination, and enable it if required. (Be sure the termination resistor is plugged in.)

f) Install the hard drive into the system, and connect the power cable.

g) Connect the 50-pin ribbon cable from the drive to the host adapter.

Step 4 Once you have the hard drive installed properly, boot your system and go into the SCSI configuration utility, just as you did when you set up the host adapter. This time select SCSI Disk Utilities from the first menu that appears.

FIGURE 12-4 Setting the ID (left) and verifying a terminating resister (right)

The auto-scan will find all the devices that are attached and will report the results in a table (see Figure 12-5).

Now that you have installed the device and the system recognizes it, you still need to configure the hard drive. Examine the scan results and enter the hard drive setup to complete the installation.

Does your hard drive show up as SCSI ID 0? _____

Highlight the drive, and press ENTER. Run the Verify test.

Did the test complete correctly? _____

Reboot your PC, allow it to go into Windows as usual, and check My Computer for your new SCSI hard drive. Also check in the Device Manager to see if the SCSI hard drive shows up.

You'll find that the installation of any SCSI device follows this same process and consists of the same steps:

a)   Physically install the SCSI device properly.

b)   Boot and go into the SCSI configuration utility.

c)   Select and run the Disk Utilities to auto-scan devices.

d)   Select the device, and complete the specific setup if necessary.

FIGURE 12-5 Reporting a successful scan for SCSI devices

e) Save and exit.

f) Reboot.

g) Load Windows drivers if necessary.

Step 5 Next, you'll add an external device:

a) Power down your PC normally.

b) Set the ID of the external device to something other than that of your hard drive or host adapter.

c) Set the termination correctly for the external device.

d) Connect the external cable, and make sure the power supply is properly connected to the device.

e) Turn on your system, go into the SCSI Disk Utilities, and scan for the device.

Does your external device show up in the scan? _____

f) Exit the SCSI Disk Utilities, and reboot.

g) Load Windows drivers if necessary.

Step 6 Now you're ready for some real SCSI-lovin' fun. Take a variety of SCSI devices, such as a CD-ROM drive, an extra hard drive, and so on, and install them one at time onto your SCSI chain.

For each device you install, follow these steps:

a) Give each device you add to the SCSI chain a unique SCSI ID.

b) Be sure only the end device in the SCSI chain is terminated. Remember, you have two SCSI chains, one internal and one external. Each chain must be terminated only once at the end of the chain.

c) Check your cable connectivity.

d) Scan the SCSI BIOS (ROM for the host adapter) for devices.

If you have several SCSI devices available, try the following configurations:

- Two internal devices, one external device

- One internal device, two external devices

- Two or more internal devices, two or more external devices

✔ **Hint**

Terminating something in the middle of the SCSI chain or not terminating the end of a chain will cause devices to work incorrectly, right? So the big question with multiple devices is, "Where are the *ends* of the chain?" Look at the SCSI configurations in Figure 12-6. It shows fairly common configurations of two and three devices and where to set termination.

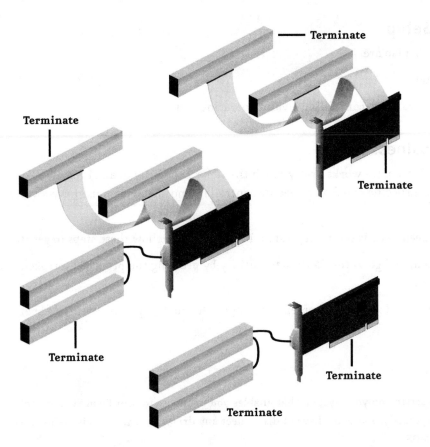

FIGURE 12-6 Correct termination settings for various SCSI configurations

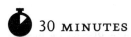 30 MINUTES

Lab Exercise 12.02: Booting from SCSI

A client has a set of PCs with mixed IDE and SCSI hard drives. The SCSI drives in this case offer more speed and size than the IDE, so the client wants to load Windows on the SCSI drives (and make them bootable). The problem is, every time he boots to the Windows CD, the setup program immediately wants to install on the IDE drives, not the SCSI drives. You've been tasked to make things right!

Learning Objectives

In this lab, you'll learn how to boot the PC system from a SCSI hard drive.

At the end of this lab, you'll be able to

• Boot from a SCSI hard drive

Lab Materials and Setup

The materials you need for this lab are

- A working computer

- An installed SCSI hard drive containing a valid operating system

Getting Down to Business

In theory, booting to a SCSI hard drive works pretty much the same as booting to an IDE drive. You must tell the BIOS to boot to a specific drive on a specific controller, and the drive must have a valid operating system.

Step 1 The first thing you need to do is set up the system BIOS properly. Follow these steps to get started:

a) Turn on your system, and go to the CMOS setup utility by pressing the proper keystroke(s) during the boot process.

b) Select the BIOS Features (or similar) screen, and adjust the Boot Sequence setting to boot from SCSI first.

✔ **Hint**

If you don't have a BIOS setting on your system that enables you to choose to boot from SCSI, disable the EIDE controllers temporarily. You don't have to disconnect any drives for this exercise—just disable the controllers in CMOS.

---

c) Save your settings and reboot the system.

Step 2 Configure the host adapter to boot from the SCSI hard drive:

a) Watch for the message to enter the SCSI configuration utility during the boot process, and press the proper keystroke(s) to open it.

b) Configure the SCSI host adapter BIOS to point to the SCSI hard drive's ID as the bootable ID. You can usually find the bootable device in the additional or advanced options (see Figures 12-5 and 12-7).

c) Save your changes, exit the SCSI configuration utility, and reboot your system.

d) Watch the messages as your system boots. If you have configured everything correctly, you should be booting to the SCSI hard drive.

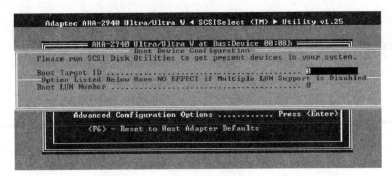

FIGURE 12-7 Setting a bootable device ID

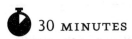 30 MINUTES

Lab Exercise 12.03: Troubleshooting SCSI

In this lab, you'll purposely set up (break and fix) various SCSI installations. By introducing controlled errors, observing the symptoms, and repairing the problems, you gain the experience to recognize many different types of problems while working in the field.

Learning Objectives

In this lab, you'll set up (break and fix) various SCSI installation scenarios.

At the end of this lab, you'll be able to

- Recognize different types of problems with SCSI installations
- Repair SCSI installation problems

Lab Materials and Setup

The materials you need for this lab are

- A working PC system
- SCSI devices and cables, as outlined in Lab Exercise 12.01

Getting Down to Business

Because you built a working SCSI system in Lab Exercise 12.01, you can use that setup to complete these troubleshooting exercises.

Step 1   Set up a SCSI chain as outlined in Lab Exercise 12.01 with at least one internal and one or more external drives.

Step 2   Create the following errors, and report the results with your combination(s) of hardware:

a)   Set the termination incorrectly.

Take the termination off one end of the chain. Does it work? Why or why not?

_____

_____

Explain what happens if you take the termination off of both ends.

_____

_____

What happens to a device on the end of a chain when you terminate something in the middle of the chain? Can you access it?

_____

_____

✔ **Hint**

To make the termination scenarios work, force your host adapter to be something other than Auto for termination. Set it on or off according to how you want the scenario to go.

---

b)   Set the SCSI IDs incorrectly.

What happens when two or more devices share an ID?

_____

_____

What happens when the host adapter and a device share an ID? Does anything work?

_____

_____

c) Try other combinations of termination errors and ID conflicts, and document the results you observe for future reference.

_____

_____

_____

_____

✖ Warning

Do not reverse the ribbon cables on SCSI devices. You can destroy both the device and the host adapter by doing so. This, as we say, would be a *bad* thing.

Lab Analysis Test

1. Sergio just installed a PCI SCSI host adapter and a single internal hard drive. The hard drive does not show up in My Computer. What is one possible reason?

_____

_____

2. You receive a phone call from Thelma, who says her system no longer boots from the SCSI hard drive since she added an external SCSI CD-ROM drive. It works fine if she disconnects the new drive. What can cause this to happen?

_____

_____

3. Sam is upset. He added a second ATA CD-ROM drive, and now the system cannot find the SCSI boot disk. What is a possible cause?

_____

_____

4. You have a 50-pin SCSI cable with six connectors. You connect the host adapter at one end of the cable, then connect four hard drives, and finally put a terminator in the last connector farthest from the host adapter. The system cannot see the third and fourth drive. Why?

_____

_____

5. For the previous question, you fix the apparent problem, but you can still see only two drives. What could be the problem now?

_____

_____

Key Term Quiz

Use the following vocabulary terms to complete the following sentences. Not all of the terms will be used.

BIOS

cable

chain

host adapter

IDs

SCSI

termination

1. A SCSI _____ can include a total of 16 devices.

2. The fastest hard drive data transfer rate is 320 MBps, using a _____ controller.

3. The devices in a SCSI chain are assigned unique _____.

4. In order for the SCSI chain to support multiple devices, it must have proper _____.

5. A SCSI _____ is always an internal component.

Chapter 13
Sound

Lab Exercises

Every PC comes with the ability to output sound, from the tinny, built-in PC speaker to state of the art surround sound. Accomplished PC techs can handle the full range, installing, configuring, and troubleshooting sound in the PC. As such, the A+ Certification exams expect you to know about sound cards and their workings.

 30 MINUTES

Lab Exercise 13.01: Installing Sound

A new client has upgraded his company's PCs, but wants to keep the high-end sound cards from the old systems. The problem is that the new motherboards have built-in sound. You need to disable the onboard sound, install the new cards, get them running correctly, and troubleshoot if you run into problems. In this lab, you'll become familiar with using and installing sound cards. A PC sound system consists of a sound card, a set of speakers, a microphone, and software drivers. In this lab exercise, you'll physically install all the components of a sound system for a PC.

Learning Objectives

This lab teaches you the basics of installing and configuring a sound card.

At the end of this lab, you'll be able to

- Remove and install a sound card

- Configure a sound card

Lab Materials and Setup

The materials you need for this lab are

- A working computer system running Windows 98, Windows Me, Windows 2000, or Windows XP

- A removable sound card and speakers properly installed and functioning (the sound drivers must either be part of the operating system in use or be available on CD or disk)

✖ Warning

Different versions of Windows handle the drivers differently, to say the least. You should have a current driver disk for your sound card handy just in case Windows decides it cannot remember your sound card!

Getting Down to Business

This lab will step you through removing, installing, and configuring a sound card.

Step 1 Begin by examining the configuration and resources currently being used by the sound card. Turn on your machine, and boot to Windows. Go to the Device Manager in the Control Panel (see Figure 13-1).

✔ **Hint**

There are several ways to access the Device Manager. In Windows 2000/XP, there's a Device Manager button on the Hardware tab of the System applet. In Windows 98/Me, the System applet has a Device Manager tab.

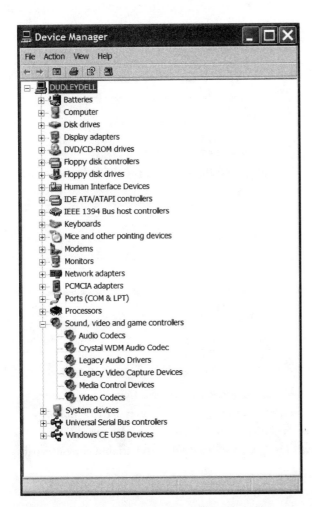

FIGURE 13-1 The Device Manager in Windows XP

Next, follow these steps:

a) Click the plus sign (+) next to Sound, Video and Game Controllers (Sound Devices in Windows 98/2000).

b) Highlight the sound card icon.

✔ Hint

The name of the sound card icon differs according to the type of sound card you have installed. A Creative Labs Soundblaster Live! card, for example, has the entry listed as "Creative SB Live! Series (WDM)." Try them all if it's not obvious at first glance.

---

c) Alternate-click and select Properties.

d) Select the Resources tab.

Verify what resources the sound is using and that there are no conflicts.

What Interrupt Requests (IRQ) are listed now? _____

What Direct Memory Access (DMA) channels are listed? _____

What Input/Output (I/O) addresses are listed? _____

e) Select the Driver tab, and record all the information available about the driver that is currently installed.

_____

_____

Step 2 Now that you've seen what resources are currently being used, the next step is to practice removing and reinstalling the sound card.

✔ Hint

This lab assumes you have a removable sound card, not onboard sound. If all you have to work with is a system with onboard sound, go into the CMOS setup utility and turn off the onboard sound. Make what observations you can and resume with step 3. When the time comes in the second half of step 3 to reinstall the sound card, just go back into CMOS and enable the onboard sound again.

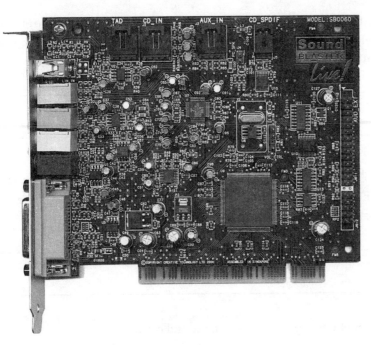

FIGURE 13-2 A typical sound card

a) Close the Device Manager and Control Panel, and properly shut down your system. Unplug the power cord.

b) Remove the case cover from your system and locate the sound card (see Figure 13-2).

What type of slot is it in? _____

c) Disconnect any cables that are attached to the sound card (both internal and external), take out the retaining screw that holds the sound card, and then carefully remove the card. Make sure you're grounded before you touch the card!

What sort of onboard connectors does it have?

_____

_____

What sort of external connectors does it have?

_____

_____

Is there a way to adjust the volume on the card? _____

Does it have jumpers? What are they used for? Look on the Internet for the answers. Search for the card manufacturer and look under its tech support for your specific model. This information is also available in the documentation for the card if you still have it around.

_____

_____

What is the brand name of the sound-processing chip? _____

Is the name on the chip different from the name of the manufacturer of the card? (Does the chip have "ESS" printed on it, for example, but the board has "Creative Labs" on it?)

_____

_____

Describe the cables you disconnected when you removed the sound card.

_____

_____

Does the card have an IDE interface on it? If so, you have a really old card. How would the IDE interface be used?

✔ Hint

In old systems that only had one IDE controller on the motherboard, how were CD-ROM drives connected when you had two hard drives in the system?

_____

_____

Step 3 With the card out of your system, turn on the machine and let it boot to the Windows Desktop. Go to the Device Manager in the Control Panel.

Expand the Sound and Audio Devices option and see if your sound card is still listed.

Did Windows automatically remove the device when the card was removed? _____

If the sound card is still listed, highlight the icon, alternate-click, and select Remove. Am I sure? Yes!

Save your changes, and shut your system off properly.

The next steps will confirm that the device has been removed:

a) Reboot your system, go to the Device Manager, and confirm that the sound device is no longer listed.

b) Shut down your system and disconnect the power cord. Insert the sound card in the same slot you removed it from, secure the board with the proper retaining screw, and connect all the cables.

c) Reboot the system. When the Plug and Play (PnP) kicks in, your system should recognize that you have added a card.

Windows will now locate the software drivers for the new hardware you installed. In fact, unless you uninstalled them, the drivers should still be on your system.

Step 4 Open the Control Panel again, and then follow these steps:

a) Double-click the System icon.

b) Select the Device Manager tab.

d) Click the plus sign (+) next to Sound and Audio Devices.

d) Highlight the Sound Card icon.

e) Click the Properties button.

f) Select the Resources tab.

Verify what resources the sound is using and that there are no conflicts.

What IRQ is listed now? _____

What DMA channels are listed? _____

What I/O addresses are listed? _____

Are the settings the same as they were in step 1 before you removed the card?

_____

_____

Go to the Drivers tab and confirm that Windows installed the same drivers in the system. If necessary, use the driver disk (or the CD) to reinstall the correct drivers.

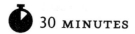 30 MINUTES

Lab Exercise 13.02: Testing Sound

This lab exercise will help you understand different ways to test and troubleshoot the basic sound card and speaker installation.

Learning Objectives

The purpose of this lab exercise is to show you how to use the Windows software to test the sound system and also use the Internet to search for useful testing tools.

At the end of this lab, you'll be able to

- Verify the sound system works

- Use the microphone to record a .wav file

Lab Materials and Setup

The materials you need for this lab are

- A working computer system running Windows 98, Windows Me, Windows 2000, or Windows XP

- A sound card, speakers, and a microphone properly installed

Getting Down to Business

Once you have installed and configured a sound card, you need to make sure everything is working. This lab steps you through some practical tests to confirm everything is working properly.

Step 1   Verify there are no conflicts with the sound installation. Look in the Device Manager for any indications of problems. Resource conflicts or incorrect drivers installed will cause the rest of this exercise to fail.

Is everything okay? _____

Step 2   Start by adjusting the speaker volume to a comfortable level.

Make sure your speakers are plugged into the proper jack on the sound card.

Is the speaker pair plugged into the AC outlet? Are there batteries to be checked?

_____

Is there a volume adjustment knob on your speakers? _____ Adjust the knob to the middle position.

Access the Control Panel.

Select the proper icon (see the following Hint) to place a Volume icon in the taskbar for easy access later.

✔ Hint

There are several ways to place the Volume icon in the taskbar so you can adjust the volume. Follow the procedure that matches your operating system:

- In Windows 98/Me, select the Multimedia icon in the Control Panel, and select the Show Volume Control on the Taskbar check box.

- In Windows 2000, select the Sounds and Multimedia icon in the Control Panel, and select the Show Volume Control on the Taskbar check box.

- In Windows XP, select the Sounds and Audio Devices icon in the Control Panel, and select the Place Volume Icon in the Taskbar check box.

Once you have the Volume icon in the taskbar, double-click it to open the volume controls, and follow these steps:

a) Check to be sure the Mute All option is not selected (see Figure 13-3).

b) Select Options | Properties.

c) Select the volume controls you want to control.

d) Close the Properties window.

e) Now adjust all the sliders to the center position.

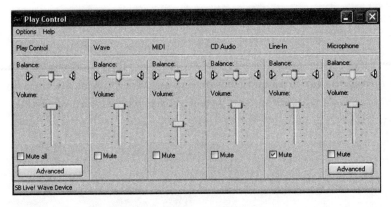

Figure 13-3 Setting the volume controls

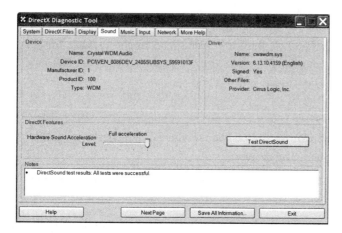

FIGURE 13-4 Using DirectX Diagnostic tool

You now have a good starting point to play sounds. Once you know the sounds are coming from the speakers, you can go back and customize the levels you desire.

Step 3   Test the speakers, and adjust the sound volume to a comfortable audible level. A good tool to use to test your sound card is the DirectX Diagnostic tool. This is the same tool you used in Chapter 11 to test video performance. Follow these steps:

a)   Click Start | Run, and enter **dxdiag**. This will launch the DirectX Diagnostic tool (see Figure 13-4).

b)   Select the Sound tab. Examine the information displayed about your sound card and drivers.

c)   Click the Test Direct Sound button. This will step through a series of tests to confirm the operation of your sound system. The Sound function will check the capability of your system's sound processor to handle such things as positional audio used for game sound effects.

d)   Select the Music tab, and click the Test Direct Music button. This will test your system's capability to play .wav and .midi files.

Step 4   The last step is to check your system's ability to record and play back. Make sure your microphone is plugged into the proper connector, and then follow these steps:

a)   Access the Sound Recorder by selecting Start | Programs | Accessories | Entertainment | Sound Recorder. What you have now is similar to an audio cassette player. The buttons are the same —Record, Play, Fast Forward, Rewind, and Stop—only they are not labeled with words but with icons (see Figure 13-5).

FIGURE 13-5 Using the Windows
Sound Recorder

b) Click the red Record button, and start talking into the microphone. Watch the graph to see that it is recording. If not, check your connections.

c) Click Stop at any time; then click Play (the forward arrow) to hear your recording.

✔ **Hint**

This a good feature to set up custom sound files to play during events. An example would be the sound file "You've got mail."

---

d) If you want to save your recordings, select File | Save As.

Step 5 You've learned to remove, install, and configure a sound card. You've also learned how to test the various parts of the sound system. Now it's time to talk about troubleshooting.

Your sound system is working, but your speakers sound a little rough. Are they "blown" out because they were overdriven with poor adjustments? You can go to this Internet site and test the response of your speakers at different frequencies:

http://www.eminent-tech.com/music/multimediatest.html

These tests will help you confirm if your speakers can still handle all the frequencies they are designed to handle.

Lab Analysis Test

1. Suddenly and for no apparent reason the speaker icon no longer shows up in the taskbar area. Where would you check to be sure it is enabled?

   _____

   _____

2. John replaced his motherboard with one that has built-in sound. He still wants to use his Creative Labs Audigy sound card. What must he do to prevent conflicts?

   _____

   _____

3. Teresa has been using her system for a long time to visit with friends in chat rooms. Lately her friends are complaining her sound quality is getting worse. What should she check first?

   _____

   _____

4. Kal is not getting any sound from his speakers. What three things should he check?

_____

_____

5. John complains about annoying sounds when he opens and closes certain programs and sometimes when he clicks his mouse. He asks you if you can make them go away. Can you?

_____

_____

Key Term Quiz

Use the following vocabulary terms to complete the following sentences. Not all of the terms will be used.

aux

compression

line-in

.mp3

sound card

Sound Recorder

speaker

.wav

1. Joe wants to record himself singing, "Hound Dog" to honor the birthday of the King. He plugs a microphone into the sound card and opens the _____, the recording software that comes with Windows.

2. Using the default tools, Windows saves such audio recordings as _____ files.

3. To join conversations in an audio chat room, you must have a _____.

4. The MP3 format is popular because of the _____ scheme it uses.

5. High-quality recordings are mostly stored in _____ files.

Chapter 14
Portable PCs

Lab Exercises

The world has gone mobile, and accomplished technicians travel right along with it. General technicians have always worked on the software side of portables, tweaking power management options to optimize battery life for the users. Working on the hardware side of portable computing devices of all stripes, however, used to be the realm of only highly specialized technicians. As portable computing devices become increasingly common and the technology inside becomes more modular, however, frontline general technicians (think A+ Certified technicians here) increasingly get the call to upgrade and repair these devices.

Most portable computers (PCs, not PDAs) have parts that a user can easily replace. You can swap out a fading nickel-cadmium (NiCD) battery for a higher-performance nickel-metal-hydride (NiMH) battery on some models, for example, or add a second battery in place of a CD-RW drive for long airplane trips. Lurking beneath access panels on the underside or below the keyboard on some models are hardware components such as RAM, a hard drive, a network card, and a modem—just like laptop batteries, these units can be easily accessed and replaced by a technician. Some laptops even have panels for replacing the video card and CPU.

In this series of labs, you'll do four things. First, you'll use the Internet to research so you can provide proper recommendations to employers and clients about the upgrades available for portable computing devices. Second, you'll open a laptop and gut it like a rainbow trout—removing and replacing RAM, the most common of all hardware upgrades. Third, you'll perform the traditional task of a portable PC technician, tweaking the power management options to optimize battery life on particular models. Finally, you'll tour a computer store to familiarize yourself with the latest and greatest portable offerings.

30 MINUTES

Lab Exercise 14.01: Researching to Provide a Proper Upgrade Recommendation

Your boss just sent word that one of your most important clients wants to extend the life of their sales force's laptop computers by upgrading rather than replacing. You've been asked to provide an upgrade track for your client. This requires you to research the laptops used by the company to determine which upgrades you can make. You have to determine whether you can add RAM, replace the hard drives, replace the aging batteries, or add docking stations to provide extra functions when the salespeople are at the home office. Get to work!

Learning Objectives

Given the manufacturer and model number of a notebook computer, you'll figure out how to upgrade your client's computers.

At the end of this lab, you'll be able to

- Determine the replacement price of a battery

- Determine memory upgrades, including the quantity and type of RAM

- Determine hard drive upgrades, including the capacity and price of a hard drive

Lab Materials and Setup

The materials you need for this lab are

- A working PC with Internet access

Getting Down to Business

Limber up your surfing fingers because you're about to spend some time on the Web. Researching information about hardware and software is something technicians do all the time. The better you are at it, the better you are at your job!

When you're searching for replacement and upgrade parts and information, always take a look at the device manufacturer's web site. Most major PC manufacturers, like Dell or IBM, have comprehensive product specification sheets available to the public on their sites. You can even order replacement parts directly from them! A popular tactic for researching upgrades is to grab the upgrade specs from the manufacturer's site and then search the Internet for the best prices. Not only are you doing your job well, but you'll be saving your company money too!

In the following steps, you'll navigate the tumultuous seas of the Internet in a quest to find the Golden Fleece of laptop battery, memory, and hard drive upgrades.

Step 1   Fire up your web browser, and surf over to the device manufacturer's web site. Try http://www.dell.com. If you can't locate that site, try http://www.batteries-store.com to get information about battery upgrades. If that site isn't available, do a Google search (http://www.google.com) for "laptop battery." Many sites sell every laptop battery imaginable. The goal of this exercise is to become familiar with using the Internet to identify parts, confirm the specifications, and purchase replacement batteries. Once you reach a suitable web site, answer the following questions:

You need replacement batteries for several Dell Inspiron 8100 PCs. What's the vendor's part number and price for this battery?

_____

_____

What's the voltage and current capacity of the battery?

_____

_____

✔ Hint

Just like any other electrical power source, batteries are rated according to voltage (9.6 V, for instance) and current capacity (2600 milli-amps per hour, or mAh). When buying laptop batteries, buy a battery that matches the voltage recommended by the manufacturer. Depending on the type of battery (NiCD, NiMH, or Li-Ion), the current capacity of replacement batteries may be greater than the original battery. This is not a problem—increased current capacity means longer run-times for your portable PC.

Step 2   Search the manufacturer's web site for information on memory. If that isn't available, flip your browser over to http://www.kahlon.com to check RAM prices and availability. If the site isn't available, do a Google search to find other web sites that sell "laptop memory." Then answer the questions on the following page.

Your client has ten Dell Inspiron 8100s with 128 MB of RAM. How much RAM can you install? How many sticks of RAM will it take to get to the maximum capacity, and how much will they cost?

_____

_____

Step 3 Stay where you landed in your search for memory upgrades. Do they have replacement hard drives available as well? If not, try http://www.kahlon.com, but now research possible hard drive upgrades for the five IBM ThinkPads the client owns. Answer this question:

The client's five IBM ThinkPad T30 2366-97U PCs have 20 GB hard drives and 256 MB of RAM. How much will it cost to upgrade each ThinkPad to a 60 GB hard drive and 1 GB of RAM?

_____

_____

 30 MINUTES

Lab Exercise 14.02: Replacing and Upgrading RAM

Your client settled on the RAM upgrades as the first step for making their laptops more usable, and you get tagged as the person to remove the old RAM and install the new. Upgrading RAM is the most common technician-performed upgrade on portable PCs and something you're likely to run into in the real world.

Learning Objectives

In this lab, you'll learn essential skills for upgrading portable PCs.

At the end of this lab, you'll be able to

- Access the RAM panel in a laptop

- Remove RAM in a laptop

- Install RAM properly in a laptop

Lab Materials and Setup

The materials you need for this lab are

- A working portable computer (one with modern SO DIMM or DDR SO DIMM modules is preferable)

- A very tiny Phillips head screwdriver

✖ Warning

Opening a portable computer can result in a non-functional portable computer. Don't use the instructor's primary work laptop for this exercise!

Getting Down to Business

You're about to open the sensitive inner portions of a portable computer, but before you do, it's a great idea to refresh your memory about avoiding electrostatic discharge (ESD). The inside of a laptop looks different from the inside of a desktop or tower case, but the contents are just as sensitive to static electricity. Watch out!

Step 1 Using your handy screwdriver or other handy tool, open the access panel for the RAM. Every portable PC offers a different way to access the RAM, so I can't give you explicit directions here. Most often, you'll find a removable plate on the bottom of the laptop secured with a tiny Phillips head screw. Some laptops require you to remove the keyboard, unscrew a heat spreader, and then access the RAM. Figure 14-1 shows a typical panel, accessible from the underside of the laptop.

Step 2 Once you have the panel open, push outward on the restraining clips on the RAM stick(s). This will cause the RAM to pop up partially (see Figure 14-2).

Step 3 Remove the RAM gently, gripping only at the noncontact edges. Place the stick(s) on an anti-static pad or in an anti-static bag.

Step 4 Install the replacement RAM into the laptop, reversing the process of removal. Place the stick(s) at an angle into the RAM slots and push firmly. Once the contacts have disappeared, press the body of the RAM into the restraining clips.

> ✔ **Hint**
>
> If you don't have new RAM to install, simply install the RAM you removed in step 3. This gives you the opportunity to practice!

Step 5 Replace the access panel.

Step 6 Power on the laptop to confirm that the new RAM is recognized and functioning properly.

FIGURE 14-1 Opening the access panel to display RAM

FIGURE 14-2 Releasing the RAM

30 MINUTES

Lab Exercise 14.03: Adjusting Power Management to Optimize Battery Life

Several of your workers have to attend a conference on the other side of the country. The conference came up on short notice, so everyone needs time to prepare, even while on the flight to the conference. You've been tasked with configuring power management on their laptops to optimize battery life so they can work as long as possible while on the plane.

Learning Objectives

In this lab, you'll adjust the power management features for a PC, a task that's vital to proper support of portable PCs.

At the end of this lab, you'll be able to

- Enable and disable power management in the CMOS

- Change power management settings in Windows

Lab Materials and Setup

The materials you need for this lab are

- A working computer with Windows 98/Me/2000/XP installed

- A BIOS that supports power management

✔ **Hint**

Having a notebook computer available is a plus.

Getting Down to Business

Windows PCs have two separate areas for power management, the CMOS setup utility and the Control Panel. You'll start with CMOS and then go to the Control Panel.

Step 1 Boot your system, and enter the CMOS Setup Utility.

✔ **Cross-Reference**

Refer to the "Power Management" section in Chapter 14 of *Mike Meyers' A+ Guide to PC Hardware* for more information on power management on portable PCs.

✔ **Hint**

If you're practicing on a regular desktop PC, keep in mind that a notebook will have two options for each adjustment: one for when the notebook is using battery power and one when it's connected to the alternating current (AC) source.

Now follow these steps:

a) Go to the Power Management Setup screen.

b) Enable power management if it's currently disabled.

c) Look at each option for common sense settings. For example, when operating on battery power, you want to configure the portable to energy efficient, thus increasing run-time.

d) Make sure the ACPI setting is enabled if the BIOS supports it.

e) Save your settings, and boot the system to the Windows Desktop.

✔ **Hint**

ACPI is short for Advanced Configuration and Power Interface, a power management specification developed by Intel, Microsoft, and Toshiba. ACPI enables the operating system to control the amount of power given to each device attached to the computer. With ACPI, the operating system can turn off peripheral devices, such as CD-ROM players, when they're not in use.

Step 2   Access the Power Options applet in the Control Panel, and make a note of your current power management settings.

_____

_____

_____

Check out the different power schemes available (this will depend on your specific system) and experiment with changing the settings to see how this affects when the monitor and hard drives turn off. Each of these schemes has adjustable times. The tabs and settings will differ depending on which version of Windows you're running. Be sure to look at them all.

Now answer these questions:

Which tab contains an option to place the Power icon in the System Tray?

_____

When do the monitor and hard drives turn off while using the Presentation scheme?

_____

✔ Hint

The Windows XP (on a notebook) Power Options Properties dialog box has five tabs: Power Schemes, Alarms, Power Meter, Advanced, and Hibernate (see Figure 14-3). You can use the Alarms tab to set the time when the battery alarm is activated. The Power Meter tab shows the percent of charge remaining in the battery.

✘ Warning

Some PCs and some components don't like standby and suspend modes. They can cause your computer to lock up. Be aware of that, and if your computer locks up, turn those settings off.

Step 3 Once you've finished experimenting, enable or disable power management as you prefer.

FIGURE 14-3 Accessing the Windows XP power options on a portable computer

 30 MINUTES

Lab Exercise 14.04: Field Trip to Play with the Latest Portable PCs

The best way to understand portable PCs is to play with one. If there isn't one available in the classroom, then this exercise is for you.

Learning Objectives

This lab will take you into the field for a little computer browsing—for educational purposes, of course!

At the end of this lab, you'll be able to

- Recognize the variations in key features among different portable PCs

Lab Materials and Setup

The materials you need for this lab are

- A local computer store or other retailer with a good selection of portable PCs you can examine

 Hint

If you don't have a store nearby, use the Web to browse a computer store such as CompUSA (http://www.compusa.com).

Getting Down to Business

Portable PCs are manufactured by a wide variety of companies and no two notebooks are created equal. Some notebooks feature a slim and lightweight profile and are designed for the busy traveler; others feature a full complement of ports and rival desktop PCs in their power and features. Take a look at all the available models and compare their features.

Step 1 Go to your local computer or office-supply store, and check out the portable PCs it has on display. Try to find a store with a variety of brands. Bring this lab manual (or a copy of the following chart) with you to record the different specs you find.

Step 2 Pick out three portables, and try to choose portables from different manufacturers. For each portable, record the following information.

Feature	Portable 1	Portable 2	Portable 3
Size/weight	_____	_____	_____
Screen type/size	_____	_____	_____
CPU	_____	_____	_____
RAM	_____	_____	_____
Pointing device(s)	_____	_____	_____
I/O ports	_____	_____	_____
PC Card slot(s)	_____	_____	_____
Hard drive	_____	_____	_____
Floppy/CD/DVD drive(s)	_____	_____	_____

Lab Analysis Test

1. Kal wants to upgrade his memory from 64 MB to the maximum amount of RAM his notebook can take. He has an Inspiron 4000 notebook. How much RAM does he need to buy?

   _____

   _____

2. Teresa complains that her Windows XP notebook turns itself off without any warning. What should she adjust?

   _____

   _____

3. What are the three most common components that are replaced or upgraded in a notebook computer?

   _____

   _____

4. During your research earlier in these exercises, which did you discover to be the most expensive—hard drives, memory, or batteries? Which component was the cheapest to replace?

_____

_____

5. Would the LCD screen or hard drives turn off, for energy conservation, if you set your power scheme to Always On and you walked away for a long period of time? Why or why not?

_____

_____

Key Term Quiz

Use the following vocabulary terms to complete the following sentences. Not all of the terms will be used.

ACPI

battery

hard drive

hibernate

memory

notebook

Power Options

Power Meter

Power Scheme

standby

1. The amount of time the hard drive will continue to spin once it's no longer being accessed is determined by the _____ setting.

2. You can use the _____ applet in the Control Panel to set the power conservation options for the notebook computer.

3. The battery, _____, and, _____ are all upgradeable laptop components.

4. The amount of power remaining in a battery can be determined by looking at the _____.

5. Software can control power consumption if _____ is turned on in the CMOS setup utility.

Chapter 15

Printers

Lab Exercises

Printers continue to be a major part of the day-to-day working environment, both at home and in the office, despite attempts to create a "paperless office." What this means is that the PC technician will have to understand the operation of several types of printers and be able to keep them in good working order. Many companies have service contracts for their more expensive printers (they're usually leased property anyway!), but there will always be printers that need a good technician's love and care.

This chapter's labs will take you through a scenario in which your boss walks into your office and tells you there are five printers on their way to you—two impact printers, two inkjet printers, and a laser printer. You need to install them so that they're accessible by anyone who needs them and make sure they work properly. You'll explore different port settings and how to alter them when you need to do so. You'll also learn about some of the key differences between the two most popular types of printers (inkjet and laser printers), and you'll load printer drivers.

 30 MINUTES

Lab Exercise 15.01: Exploring Configuration Settings

The two most common ports used in connecting a printer to a PC are the Universal Serial Bus (USB) and parallel ports. It just so happens that these are the ones your five new printers will be connecting through! In this lab, you'll look at these two and walk through the process of enabling and configuring the ports in the BIOS.

Learning Objectives

In this lab, you'll explore the different configuration settings that are available in your PC's CMOS setup utility.

At the end of this lab, you'll be able to

- Enable and configure common ports in the basic input/output services (BIOS)
- Locate information about the parallel port in Device Manager

Lab Materials and Setup

The materials you need for this lab are

- A working computer with Windows 98/Me/2000/XP

 Hint

> The steps assume you have Windows XP and will only vary slightly for other versions of Windows, mostly in the paths to get to certain configuration windows. By now you should be quite familiar with the different paths used by various versions of Windows.

Getting Down to Business

First, take a look at the ports in your CMOS setup utility. You may never need to use this, but it's really helpful to know, and the A+ exam expects you'll be familiar with the information.

Step 1 Boot your PC, and go into the CMOS setup utility. Find the settings for your USB and parallel ports. They'll most likely be under a heading such as Integrated Peripherals (see Figure 15-1).

✖ **Warning**

> When making changes to the system resources in both CMOS and Device Manager, be sure to first write down the current settings. If your changes don't work, you can always return them to the original settings that did.

Do you have a USB controller? _____

Is the USB controller set to Enable or Disable? _____ (It must be enabled for an attached printer to work via the USB cable. Some motherboards offer a setting to disable a USB controller.)

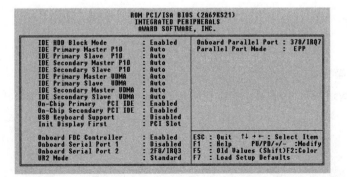

FIGURE 15-1 Accessing the CMOS—Integrated Peripherals

How many parallel ports do you have? _____

What resources are the parallel port using? _____

Is there a way to select the parallel port mode of operation? _____

How many different parallel modes are supported? List them.

_____

_____

Which mode would put the least amount of strain on the central processing unit (CPU)?

_____

✔ **Hint**

Which mode uses Direct Memory Access (DMA)?

✔ **Cross-Reference**

Refer to the "Printer Connectivity" section in Chapter 15 of *Mike Meyers' A+ Guide to PC Hardware* for help identifying parallel port modes and their differences and similarities.

Step 2   Make the following changes in CMOS, and observe any effect on hardware installed on the parallel ports. Make sure you have drivers or parallel devices handy because making changes at the CMOS level can make Windows unhappy! (You might need to reinstall drivers.)

- Parallel Port = I/O Address 378 and IRQ 7
- Parallel Port Mode = ECP or ECP+EPP
- DMA = 3
- EPP Mode = EPP1.7

Exit CMOS properly, saving your changes.

Step 3   Reboot your system to the Windows Desktop, and access Device Manager in the Control Panel to verify that the resources are assigned.

Confirm the resources allocated to the parallel port by following these steps:

a)   Click the plus sign (+) next to Ports (COM and LPT).

b)   Highlight the LPT port in the list, and click Properties.

c)   Select the Resources tab.

      What are the I/O and IRQ settings for this port? _____

d)   Click OK to close the Properties dialog box.

Step 4   Verify the resources again by accessing the list of resources used in Device Manager:

a)   From the Device Manager, select View.

b)   Select Resources by Type.

c)   Expand the groups as needed by clicking the plus sign (+) next to the desired resource.

      What DMA is assigned to the ECP printer port? _____

      What I/O addresses are assigned to the ECP printer port? _____

      What IRQ is assigned to the ECP printer port? _____

✔ **Hint**

If there's no IRQ listed, it may be by design. Look at the ports (COM and LPT) in Device Manager, and display the properties of the ECP printer port. Click the Settings tab—do you see the selection for never using an interrupt? Change the selection to Use Any Interrupt Assigned to the Port, and verify the resources again as outlined previously in the previous step.

Verify all of your settings, and close the Device Manager, Control Panel, and My Computer to return to the Desktop.

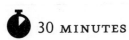 30 MINUTES

Lab Exercise 15.02: Examining Types of Printers

There's an enormous amount of information on the Internet about printers. All of the top printer manufacturers, like HP, Lexmark, and Canon, have web sites that can provide insight about modern printers. As a PC technician, you'll need to visit these sites for information about your new printers and to download the most current drivers for those printers.

Learning Objectives

In this lab, you'll compare the features of inkjet and laser printers using the Internet.

At the end of this lab, you'll be able to

- Recognize the key differences between impact, inkjet, and laser printers

- Identify and visit web sites on the Internet dedicated to printers and printer troubleshooting

Lab Materials and Setup

The materials you need for this lab are

- A working computer with Windows 98/Me/2000/XP installed

- A connection to the Internet

- Access to either an inkjet or laser printer

✔ Hint

A trip to your local computer store or other retailer with a good selection of printers would be beneficial for a general knowledge of printers.

✖ Warning

You must have access to the Internet for this exercise. If there's no access or the sites are down, refer to Chapter 15 of *Mike Meyers' A+ Guide to PC Hardware* for a review.

Getting Down to Business

Fire up your favorite web browser and head out on the Information Superhighway. The Internet is just chock-full of helpful information about printers.

✔ Hint

Web sites have the annoying tendency to either disappear or lose the information that was once relevant to a particular subject. If any of the links in this lab manual are no longer active or don't seem to contain information relevant to the exercise in question, please direct your browser to http://www.mikemeyersaplus.com to find an updated list of links and modified lab exercises.

Step 1   To find information about inkjet printers, access the following web site to complete this step: http://computer.howstuffworks.com/inkjet-printer.htm/printable.

If this link doesn't work, you can also do a Google search and look for information about how printers work.

What's the major difference between impact and non-impact printers?

_____

_____

In an inkjet printer, what two parts move the print head back and forth across the front of the paper?

_____

_____

Describe the two ways in which the droplets of ink are formed in inkjet printers.

_____

_____

The type of paper used in an inkjet printer greatly influences the quality of the image produced. What are the two main characteristics of inkjet printer paper that affect the image the most?

_____

_____

Step 2   For information about laser printers, access this site to complete this step: http://www.howstuffworks.com/laser-printer.htm/printable.
Do a Google search or refer to the textbook if this site isn't available.

What's the primary principle at work in a laser printer?

_____

_____

What moves the image from the drum to the paper?

_____

_____

Printer Control Language (PCL) and PostScript are both examples of what?

_____

_____

What's toner? Is it an ink, wax, or something else?

_____

_____

Step 3   Put these steps in the printing process of a laser printer in the correct order (don't forget to reference the textbook as well):

Charge	_____
Clean	_____
Toner	_____
Fuse	_____
Transfer	_____
Write	_____

Step 4   If you have access to a laser printer, open it and carefully examine the insides. Also read the printer manual for details on the specifications. Access the manufacturer's web site for additional information.

If you don't have access to a laser printer, go to your local office supply or computer store and ask a salesperson to show you the differences between various impact, inkjet (black and white as well as color), and laser printers.

Look inside your laser printer.

What parts are easily removable and replaceable?

_____

_____

FIGURE 15-2 Viewing a toner cartridge with its photosensitive drum exposed

Practice removing and reinserting the toner (see Figure 15-2) and paper.

✖ **Warning**

Remember to turn the printer off before removing anything but the toner or paper. Also, be careful not to spill any toner inside the printer.

Look at the manual or the manufacturer's web site for these specifications. Answer all the following questions you can about your printer:

How much random access memory (RAM) can it hold? _____

How much effect does the amount of RAM have on the cost of a new printer? _____

Are the drum and toner separate, or are they one replaceable part? _____

Speed of the printer (pages per minute) _____

Quality of the output (resolution) _____

Number and types of ink cartridges _____

Price of a new printer _____

Cost per page _____

✔ **Hint**

Most inkjet (and even laser) printers are priced very low so they're affordable to buy initially. Using them is another question. Ask yourself about the cost of the ink and how many pages it'll print. This calculation will amaze you. They're not so cheap after all.

What can you conclude from your research about the true total cost of printing including consumables?

_____

_____

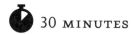 30 MINUTES

Lab Exercise 15.03: Installing a Printer

The key to a successful printer installation is having the correct software drivers. You'll certainly need these when you install those five printers.

Learning Objectives

In this lab, you'll install a printer and change its settings.

At the end of this lab, you'll be able to

- Recognize the variations in key features of laser printers

- Install a laser printer in Windows

- Change laser printer settings in Windows

Lab Materials and Setup

The materials you need for this lab are

- A working computer with Windows 98/Me/2000/XP installed

- A laser printer for installation (or you can skip step 1)

Getting Down to Business

These days, installing a printer is a fairly straightforward task. This is good because you'll probably do your fair share of it as a computer technician.

Step 1   If you have a laser printer, start here. (If you don't, skip to step 2.)

Connect the printer to your system via a parallel or USB port, and turn on the printer, then the PC. As the boot sequence progresses, the Plug and Play feature will locate the printer and install it for you. Follow the instructions on the screen.

✔ **Hint**

Here's the twist. If your printer is older than your operating system, it'll install the printer drivers with little interaction on your part. If the printer is newer than your operating system, then you'll need to have the driver CD or disk handy because the system will stop and ask you for it.

Step 2 If you don't have a laser printer, start here:

a) Access the Printer applet.

b) For Windows 98, select My Computer | Printers. For Windows 2000, select Start | Settings | Printers. For Windows XP, select Start | Printers and Faxes.

c) Click the Add Printer icon. A wizard should pop up on to the screen. Click Next to proceed.

d) You want to install a printer attached to your PC so select the option for "Local printer attached to this computer" (see Figure 15-3).

e) Follow the steps through the Printer Wizard by selecting LPT1 and then a printer from the list of printers or your driver CD.

✖ **Warning**

If you weren't able to install a printer for this exercise, don't print a test page. You'll receive some interesting messages if you do.

Once you've installed the printer, open the Printers folder in the Control Panel, alternate-click the new printer's icon, and select Properties.

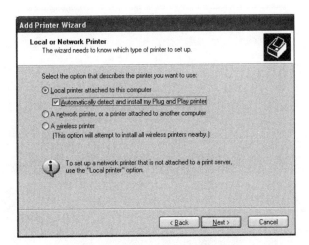

FIGURE 15-3 Installing a local printer

You'll see the various tabs and options depending on your printer. I used the Hewlett-Packard 970CSE from the built-in drivers list. Check each of your tabs to see the information available and the features you can change:

General   Description, preferences, and print test

Sharing   To share or not to share, that is the question.

Ports   Additional ports to assign the printer

Advanced   Spooling, separator page, and print defaults

Color Management   Automatic or manual

Security   Permissions

Device Settings   Additional paper trays and features

Services   Change the print cartridges

✔ **Hint**

You should know how to navigate all the previous steps for all the different Windows versions (Windows 98/Me/2000/XP) for the A+ exams.

Lab Analysis Test

1. Name two places where the IRQ and I/O address can be adjusted for the parallel printer port.

_____

_____

2. Teresa is using Windows XP and just purchased a printer from a friend. When she installs it using the original driver CD that came with the printer, it won't install properly. Why?

_____

_____

3. John installed a parallel scanner on the same port with his laser printer. The system now seems sluggish when he scans and prints documents. What did he forget to do?

_____

_____

4. Kal did everything according to the book to install his new USB printer. He installed the software drivers first and then rebooted the system with the printer attached. The printer wasn't found. Why?

_____

_____

5. Why are laser toner cartridges so expensive?

_____

_____

Key Term Quiz

Use the following vocabulary terms to complete the following sentences. Not all of the terms will be used.

DMA

ECP

impact

inkjet

laser

pages/month

primary corona

toner

transfer corona

USB

1. The part of the laser printer that actually causes the toner image to be created on the paper is the _____.

2. To utilize the extended capabilities of the parallel port, you must turn on _____.

3. The duty cycle of a printer is known as the _____.

4. The printer that spits ink onto the paper as a(n) _____ printer.

5. Printers with platens are _____ printers.

Chapter 16
Networking

Lab Exercises

There's no doubt about it—a PC technician *will* have networking issues to work through at some point. Whether it's a three-computer, home-based local area network (LAN), a public WiFi access point, a large company with thousands of connected devices, or the Web itself, networks have become as common as PCs. This is why CompTIA now includes questions about the basic workings of networks on the A+ Core Hardware exam.

All too often, an A+ technician is called upon to be a network "guru." This happens frequently, especially in smaller companies that can't afford to hire multiple people to support both the network *and* the PCs.

In this chapter's labs, you've been hired to work for a small company that has just (finally) decided to build a network in their office. You need to have a working understanding of network hardware, as well as some good troubleshooting tools for when things don't work quite right.

 30 MINUTES

Lab Exercise 16.01: Identifying Local Area Network Hardware

Your boss decides to network the eight computers in your office, and he wants your ideas about purchasing the right equipment. Your company is a small one, so the task is quite doable, but you need to make sure you know what you're talking about before you give your report.

Learning Objectives

In this lab, you'll familiarize yourself with networking hardware.

At the end of this lab, you'll be able to

- Identify different kinds of network cabling
- Identify different network interface cards (NICs)
- Identify different types of network hubs
- Identify different wireless networking devices

Lab Materials and Setup

The materials you need for this lab are

- Access to a PC running Windows

- Access to a working local area network and the Internet (you may have demonstration devices provided by your instructor)

Getting Down to Business

One of the best ways to find out what a network is made of is to look at all of its pieces. Even then, however, it may be necessary to access a manufacturer's web site to see, for instance, if the "hub" you're using is really a hub or a switch.

Step 1 If you have access to a LAN (the classroom computer lab network, a friend's home network, or your company's network), spend some time exploring the physical hardware connections and devices.

> ✖ **Warning**
>
> Don't disconnect anything and be careful while probing around. One small mistake, like removing a cable or turning off the wrong device, can disrupt the entire network. If you're using the classroom network, ask the instructor what you can and can't remove while you make closer inspections of the cables and devices.

> ✔ **Cross-Reference**
>
> Be sure to check out Chapter 16 of *Mike Meyers' A+ Guide to PC Hardware* for help identifying network cables and connectors. It's a good idea to have the textbook handy while you progress through this lab.

What sort of cabling does the network use, or is it wireless? Is it twisted-pair cable or coaxial cable? Does it use "T" connectors? Are the cable ends BNC or RJ-45? Describe the physical layout of the LAN here.

_____

_____

_____

_____

FIGURE 16-1 A network interface card (NIC)

What sort of NICs do the machines have? Describe the back of a card. Does it have a single connector or a combination of connectors (see Figure 16-1)? Does it have an antenna? Is there a link and/or activity LED? Which of the LEDs is on steadily? Which is flashing? Describe the NIC here.

_____

_____

Step 2 Hubs and switches are very much a part of every network.

Are the PCs connected with a single cable (crossover cable limited to two PCs), or are they connected to a hub or switch (see Figure 16-2)? Is part of the network wireless? What is the model number of the network hub or switch? Who manufactures it? How many devices can be attached? Record your findings here.

_____

_____

FIGURE 16-2 A LAN hub with multiple cables/devices attached

Is the hub or switch a standard single speed (10BaseT, for instance) device, or can it handle multiple speeds (10/100/1000 Mbps)? Does it have wireless capabilities? If it isn't apparent or printed on the cabinet, ask the instructor or the network administrator.

_____

_____

Step 3   Are you going to have a wireless network or wireless devices in your network? Do you plan on installing a wireless network sometime in the near future? Follow these steps:

   a)   Go to http://www.linksys.com/products/; Linksys has an excellent selection of wireless products.

✔ Hint

Web sites have the annoying tendency to either disappear or lose the information that was once relevant to a particular subject. If any of the links in this lab manual are no longer active or don't seem to contain information relevant to the exercise in question, please direct your browser to www.mikemeyersaplus.com to find an updated list of links and/or modified lab exercises.

   b)   Choose the Access Points, Routers & Gateways link, then choose WRT54G, and finally select Product Data Sheet.

   What's the WRT54G? Is it a router, switch, or wireless access point? Explain your answer.

   _____

   _____

   c)   Look at the Wireless Network Adapters section of the Linksys site.

   Would you use the WMP54G or WMP11 NIC or both in your network with a WRT54G? Explain your answer.

   _____

   _____

✔ Hint

When researching wireless compatibility issues, always look at the product data or specification sheets of the devices to see if they'll work together.

 30 MINUTES

Lab Exercise 16.02: Installing a Network Interface Card

You have been hired as a technical support specialist for a small business that wants to network their office. Your first task is to gather the appropriate hardware and tools, install NICs in their computers, and verify that the NICs work properly.

Learning Objectives

In this lab, you'll install a NIC in a computer and then connect it to a working network.

At the end of this lab, you'll be able to

- Physically install a NIC

- Verify that the NIC is operational

Lab Materials and Setup

The materials you need for this lab are

- Screwdriver

- A Windows PC with an available PCI slot

- A known-good NIC

- Drivers for the NIC

- A known-good Ethernet cable

- A working network (can be as simple as a hub or switch and a second PC plugged into the hub or switch)

Getting Down to Business

It's time to limber up your screwdriver hand and break out the anti-static wrist strap. You're ready to install some hardware!

✔ **Cross-Reference**

To review the procedure for physically installing an expansion card, refer to the "Installing Expansion Cards" section of Chapter 5 of *Mike Meyers' A+ Guide to PC Hardware*.

Step 1   Turn off and unplug the PC, open the case, and install the NIC in the available PCI slot.

Step 2   Plug the Ethernet cable into the NIC and into your hub or switch.

Step 3   Turn on your PC and boot into Windows. Watch while Windows detects the NIC. It will either install the appropriate drivers or prompt you to insert a disk containing the drivers if it doesn't recognize the NIC. When Windows finishes the installation, it may prompt you to restart the PC. Restart if necessary. Note that Windows XP indicates a new piece of hardware it supports with only a small pop-up window in the lower-right corner of your screen.

Even if Windows finds drivers, they may not be the most current ones, so if Windows did an automatic driver install, go to the Device Manager, expand Network Adapters, and double-click your newly installed NIC to check its Properties. Click the Drivers tab to see what version of the drivers Windows installed.

If you have a more recent driver than the one Windows used, install it.

Step 4   Return to the Device Manager, expand Network Adapters, and double-click your NIC again to check its Properties. The Properties dialog box should display a message that the NIC is working properly.

Step 5   Examine the NIC and hub/switch for valid link lights. Link lights are the green or orange LEDs on most network hardware. They should be on and possibly blinking irregularly to show good connectivity between the NIC and the hub or switch.

If the link lights are not lit up, verify your connectivity. Do you have a known-good cable? Is the port on the hub or switch good? Is the cable fully plugged in to both the NIC and the hub or switch?

If you have good link lights, then the hardware portion of installing a NIC and connecting it to a network is pretty much done. You need to configure software settings to go any further, so let's turn there now.

 30 MINUTES

Lab Exercise 16.03: Configuring Network Settings

Aside from the physical, you need three more pieces installed, configured, or enabled to get a fully functional network: client software, networking protocol, and sharing. This lab steps out of the realm of pure hardware and into operating system technologies briefly.

Learning Objectives

In this lab, you'll install and configure various software to make your network hardware functional.

At the end of the lab, you'll be able to

- Set up a simple LAN

Lab Materials and Setup

The materials you need for this lab are

- A functional PC with a NIC installed, running Windows 98 or later

- A network (at least a hub or switch connected to a second machine running Windows 98 or later)

Getting Down to Business

Microsoft designed Windows to run in a networked environment, so by default the OS has quite a bit of networking software installed and configured. Don't be surprised if your PC already has the same software installed and configured that this lab covers.

Step 1   The first thing you need to do is install Client for Microsoft Networks. In Windows XP, go to Control Panel and double-click the Network Connections icon. Alternate-click your Local Area Connection (if you have multiple network adapters in a single machine, there may be more than one connection), and select Properties. Select the General tab.

If you're using Windows 9x, go to Control Panel, double-click the Network icon, and select the Configuration tab. In Windows 2000/XP, go to Control Panel, double-click Network and Dial-Up Connections, and alternate-click your Local Area Connection.

You should find the following components listed in a selection window. Your system may have others as well.

Client   Client for Microsoft Networks (default**)**

Protocol   TCP/IP (default in most versions of Windows)

Service   File and Print Sharing for Microsoft Networks

If you don't have the Client for Microsoft Networks installed, now's your chance! Click the Install button and select Client from the Select Network Component Type dialog box. Click Add and Windows will open the Select Network Client dialog box. From the list of available clients, select Client for Microsoft Networks and then click OK.

→ **Note**

If you have the Client for Microsoft Networks installed already, skip to step 2.

Earlier versions of Windows might require a valid Windows installation CD-ROM and a reboot. Give Windows what it wants and meet me back at the Properties for your Local Area Connection.

Step 2   The second thing you have to do is install a network protocol. To network two or more PCs successfully, they have to run the same protocol. What protocol(s) does Windows have installed already? If necessary, install TCP/IP. Use the default configurations unless told otherwise by your instructor.

✔ **Hint**

Computers on a TCP/IP network have to have a unique IP address that follows certain conventions. Starting with Windows 98, Microsoft included a feature called Automatic Private IP Addressing (APIPA) that, as the name would suggest, automatically sets up a PC with a unique IP address. Theoretically, you can plug two PCs into a hub and, within a few minutes, they'll be able to communicate properly. The cool part about APIPA is that it works!

Step 3   At this point, you're ready to enable File and Printer Sharing so you can share and access shared resources. Go to the LAN Properties and install or simply enable File and Printer Sharing.

Step 4   Test your connection using the ping command from the command prompt. Ping broadcasts a signal that essentially says, "Hey, Machine X, if you can hear me, answer!"

To do a successful ping, first determine the IP address used by each lab machine. At the machine, get to a command prompt (select Start | Run and type **cmd** or **command**, depending on the version of Windows) and type **ipconfig**. Press ENTER and note the IP address. If you use APIPA, the number should be something like 169.254.*x.x.*

Go to another machine and access the command line. Then type **ping** followed by the IP address for the first machine. Then press ENTER. You should see something like this:

```
C:\Documents and Settings\michaelm>ping 169.254.0.7

Pinging 169.254.0.7 with 32 bytes of data:

Reply from 169.254.0.7: bytes=32 time<1ms TTL=128
Reply from 169.254.0.7: bytes=32 time<1ms TTL=128
Reply from 169.254.0.7: bytes=32 time<1ms TTL=128
Reply from 169.254.0.7: bytes=32 time<1ms TTL=128

Ping statistics for 169.254.0.7:
    Packets: Sent = 4, Received = 4, Lost = 0 <0% loss>,
Approximate round trip times in milliseconds:
    Minimum = 0ms, Maximum = 0ms, Average = 0ms
```

If you don't have the proper connectivity or your network software settings have a flaw, you'll get a Time Out error when you run ping. Go through steps 1–3 again to verify everything is connected correctly, changing settings or hardware as you troubleshoot.

1 HOUR

Lab Exercise 16.04: Troubleshooting Network Connections

Once you've installed the network, it's time to sit back and wait for the inevitable calls: somebody can't access the network or a resource on the network and they need you to fix it!

For the A+ exam and as a technician, you need to be able to troubleshoot networks in Windows 9x/Me/NT/2000/XP. In this lab, you'll create hardware problems and observe the resulting symptoms, so you'll be able to recognize them when you see them in the field.

Learning Objectives

In this lab, you'll create network connection problems and observe the resulting symptoms.

At the end of this lab, you'll be able to

- Troubleshoot network connection problems

Lab Materials and Setup

The materials you need for this lab are

- At least two PCs with working NICs and correct drivers installed

- A network hub

- Known-good Ethernet cables

Getting Down to Business

Start by setting up and networking the computers. This means making sure that the NICs are properly installed, that the systems are properly configured for NetBEUI or TCP/IP (Windows XP drops support for NetBEUI), and that the systems are connected to a network hub or switch using known-good Ethernet cabling. If you've done the labs in this chapter in sequence, you should have your network ready to go. Now you can start breaking things and see what happens!

> ✔ **Hint**
>
> If possible, do this lab exercise in both Windows networking situations—NetBEUI and TCP/IP— explained in the following steps. If you only have Windows XP, be sure you understand how to troubleshoot connections on NetBEUI networks.

Step 1   On each system you're using for this exercise, go to Device Manager and verify that the correct NIC drivers are installed. Reinstall the driver if necessary.

✔ **Hint**

Throughout the lab exercises, you're told to "go to the Control Panel" or "go to Device Manager." If you have any questions about the path to use for various versions of Windows, refer to the instructions in Lab Exercise 5.03.

Step 2   Verify that the necessary network services are installed on each of the networked systems. In Windows 2000/XP, go to the Control Panel and double-click the Network Connections icon. Alternate-click your Local Area Connection (if you have multiple network adapters in a single machine, there may be more than one connection), and select Properties. Select the General tab.

If you're using Windows 9x/Me, go to the Control Panel, double-click Network, and select the Configuration tab. In Windows 2000/XP, go to the Control Panel, double-click Network and Dial-Up Connections, and alternate-click your Local Area Connection.

Step 3   Verify that the systems have computer names and belong to a workgroup, so they can be recognized by the network and access network resources. In Windows XP, go to the Control Panel, double-click System, and select the Computer Name tab. In Windows 2000, the information is on the Network Identification tab.

In Windows 9x/Me, you must open the Control Panel, double-click Network, and then choose the Identification tab. Windows 9x/Me also has an Access Control tab where you can set controls for access to shared resources.

Step 4   Set up the network hub and connect the systems you're using for this exercise. Verify that the systems can see each other through the network hub or switch.

If you're using NetBEUI exclusively, look in My Network Places (or Network Neighborhood if you're using Windows 9x) for the other PC(s) on the network. If you're using TCP/IP, use ping as described in Lab Exercise 16.03 to confirm proper setup.

Step 5   Now that you've confirmed that your systems are successfully networked, create some problems. Start by unplugging one of the systems from the hub or switch. What happens?

Record what you see when you check the network on the disconnected machine.

NetBEUI:

_____

TCP/IP:

_____

Record what you see when you check the network on a connected machine.

NetBEUI:

_____

TCP/IP:

_____

Step 6 Now plug the disconnected system back in, but not where it was before—plug it into the hub's uplink port. What happens?

Record what you see when you check the network on the disconnected machine.

NetBEUI:

_____

TCP/IP:

_____

Record what you see when you check the network on a connected machine.

NetBEUI:

_____

TCP/IP:

_____

Step 7 Now plug the disconnected system back in properly, and then unplug power from the hub or switch. What happens?

Record what you see when you check the link lights on a connected machine.

NetBEUI:

_____

TCP/IP:

_____

Record what you see when you check the network on a connected machine.

NetBEUI:

_____

TCP/IP:

_____

Plug the hub back in. What happens?

Record what you see when you check the link lights on a connected machine.

NetBEUI:

_____

TCP/IP:

_____

Record what you see when you check the network on a connected machine.

NetBEUI:

_____

TCP/IP:

_____

Lab Analysis Test

1. Ted's boss tells him to go check Carson's computer because he's having trouble accessing the network. Ted suspects it's the newly installed NIC. How can Ted tell if Carson's NIC is operational by simply viewing the installed card?

2. Jane set up a small network of five PCs connected to a central switch. When she boots the PCs, all of them seem to have proper physical connectivity, but one machine simply won't show up in My Network Places of all the other machines, nor can it access or see any other machine. What should Jane check to troubleshoot the problem?

3. Dave picked up a pair of Ethernet network cards to install two new machines onto his company's 10BaseT Ethernet network. When he got to the office, he noted that the connectors on the back of the NICs looked like cable connectors rather than phone jacks, even though the packaging on the cards clearly stated Ethernet. What's the problem?

4. Eduardo has a PC that keeps losing its network connection. The little XP notification keeps popping up that "A network cable is unplugged." When he checks the back of the PC, he sees that the cable is firmly attached. What could the problem be?

5. Jill bought a new Windows XP computer and attached it to her Windows 98 network of four PCs running NetBEUI and 100BaseT. For some reason, the new PC does not show up at all on the network. What could the problem be?

Key Term Quiz

Use the following vocabulary terms to complete the following sentences. Not all of the terms will be used.

crossover cable

Device Manager

hub

network applet

NIC

ping

RJ-45

router

switch

wireless

1. You can use a(n) _____ to directly connect two systems (but no more) without needing a hub.

2. A(n) _____ network configuration can be ad hoc or infrastructure.

3. You can use the _____ command to verify connectivity between two machines on a network.

4. To check the version of a network adaptor's driver, check its Properties in _____.

5. Ethernet network cables use _____ connectors.

Glossary

Numerals

1.44 MB   The storage capacity of a typical 3.5-inch floppy disk.

10BaseT   An Ethernet LAN designed to run on UTP cabling. 10BaseT runs at 10 megabits per second. The maximum length for the cabling between the NIC and the hub (or switch, repeater, etc.) is 100 meters. It uses baseband signaling. No industry standard spelling exists, so sometimes written 10BASE-T or 10Base-T.

100BaseT   A generic term for any Ethernet cabling system that is designed to run at 100 megabits per second on UTP cabling. It uses baseband signaling. No industry standard spelling exists, so it's sometimes written 100BASE-T or 100Base-T.

2.1   Speaker setup consisting of two stereo speakers combined with a subwoofer.

3.5-inch floppy drive format   All modern floppy disk drives are of this size; the format was introduced 1986 and is one of the longest surviving pieces of computer hardware.

30-pin SIMM   An obsolete memory package that utilized 30 contacts to connect to the motherboard and required a whole bank to be filled before the memory was recognized.

34-pin ribbon cable   This type of cable is used by floppy disk drives.

40-pin ribbon cable   This type of cable is used to attached EIDE devices (such as hard disk drives) or ATAPI devices (such as CD-ROMs) to a system.

5.1   Five speakers and a subwoofer.

5.25-inch floppy drive format   The predecessor to the modern 3.5-inch floppy drive format; very rarely used currently.

50-pin high density HD cable   External cable for SCSI-2 devices.

50-pin ribbon cable   Also called a **Type A cable**. A type of ribbon cable used for connecting internal SCSI-1 and SCSI-2 devices.

68-pin high density HD cable   External cable for wide SCSI-2 and SCSI-3 devices.

68-pin ribbon cable   A type of cable that connects internal SCSI devices. There are two types of 68-pin ribbon cables: an obsolete Type B used in conjunction with a 50-pin Type A cable to connect early SCSI-2 devices, and a P type that can be used singularly.

72-pin SIMM   An obsolete memory package that utilized 72 contacts to connect to the motherboard, replacing 30-pin SIMMs and eliminating some of the issues with banking.

802.11b   A wireless networking standard that operates in 2.4-GHz band with a theoretical maximum throughput of 11 Mbps.

802.11g   The latest-and-greatest version of 802.11, it has data transfer speeds equivalent to 802.11a, up to 54 Mbps, with the wider 300-foot range of 802.11b, and it is backward-compatible with 802.11b.

A

Access speed   The amount of time needed for the DRAM to supply the Northbridge with any requested data.

ACPI (Advanced Configuration and Power Interface)   A power management specification that far surpasses its predecessor, APM, by providing support for hot-swappable devices and better control of power modes.

Active Matrix   Also called **TFT (Thin Film Transistor)**. A type of liquid crystal display that replaced the passive matrix technology used in most portable computer displays.

Active termination   A method for terminating fast/wide SCSI that uses voltage regulators in lieu of resistors.

Address bus   The wires leading from the CPU to the memory controller chip (chipset) that enable the CPU to address RAM. Also used by the CPU for I/O addressing. An internal electronic channel from the microprocessor to Random Access Memory, along which the addresses of memory storage locations are transmitted. Like a post office box, each memory location has a distinct number or address; the address bus provides the means by which the microprocessor can access every location in memory.

Administrator account   A user account, created when the OS is first installed, that is allowed complete, unfettered access to the system without restriction. Think of this account as the "god" account.

AGP (Accelerated Graphics Port)   A 32/64-bit expansion slot designed by Intel specifically for video that runs at 66 MHz and yields a throughput of 254 Mbps, at least. Later versions (2X, 4X, 8X) give substantially higher throughput.

Alternating current (AC)   A type of electricity where the flow of electrons alternates direction, back and forth, in a circuit.

Amperes (amps or A)   The unit of measure for amperage, or electrical current.

API (Application Programming Interface)   A software definition that describes operating system calls for application software; conventions defining how a service is invoked.

APM (Advanced Power Management)   The BIOS routines that enable the CPU to turn on and off selected peripherals.

AT (Advanced Technology)   The model name of the second- generation, 80286-based IBM computer. Many aspects of the AT, such as the BIOS, CMOS, and expansion bus, have become *de facto* standards in the PC industry. The physical organization of the components on the motherboard is called the *AT form factor*.

ATA (AT Attachment)   A type of hard drive and controller. ATA was designed to replace the earlier ST506 and ESDI drives without requiring replacement of the AT BIOS—hence, AT attachment. These drives are more popularly known as IDE drives. (*See* ST506, ESDI, and IDE.) The **ATA/33** standard has drive transfer speeds up to 33 Mbps; the **ATA/66** up to 66 Mbps; the **ATA/100** up to 100 Mbps; and the **ATA/133** up to 133 Mbps. (*See* Ultra DMA.)

ATA/ATAPI-6 Data transfer standard for parallel drives; ATA-6 hard drives and controllers can handle transfer speeds up to 100 Mbps as long as an 80-wire cable is used.

ATAPI (ATA Packet Interface) A series of standards that enable mass storage devices other than hard drives to use the IDE/ATA controllers. Extremely popular with CD-ROM drives and removable media drives like the Iomega ZIP drive. (*See* EIDE.)

ATX (AT eXtended) The popular motherboard form factor, which generally replaced the AT form factor.

AUTORUN.INF A file included on some CD-ROMs that automatically launches a program or installation routine when the CD-ROM is inserted into a CD-ROM drive.

B

Baby AT A derivative of the AT form factor with a much smaller footprint. *See also* AT (Advanced Technology).

Backside bus The set of wires that connect the CPU to Level 2 cache. First appearing in the Pentium Pro, most modern CPUs have a special backside bus. Some buses, such as that in the later Celeron processors (300A and beyond), run at the full speed of the CPU, whereas others run at a fraction. Earlier Pentium IIs, for example, had backside buses running at half the speed of the processor. *See also* Frontside bus and External data bus.

Bandwidth A piece of the spectrum occupied by some form of signal, such as television, voice, fax data, etc. Signals require a certain size and location of bandwidth in order to be transmitted. The higher the bandwidth, the faster the signal transmission, allowing for a more complex signal such as audio or video. Because bandwidth is a limited space, when one user is occupying it, others must wait their turn. Bandwidth is also the capacity of a network to transmit a given amount of data during a given period.

Bank The total number of SIMMs that can be accessed simultaneously by the chipset. The "width" of the external data bus divided by the "width" of the SIMM sticks.

Base I/O address The base I/O address refers to the first address in a device's I/O address set. Techs commonly refer to the full set of addresses by using only the base address and drop the leading zeros. A sound card that used the I/O address range of 0330 to 033F, for example, would be said to use I/O 330.

Baud One analog cycle on a telephone line. In the early days of telephone data transmission, the baud rate was often analogous to bits-per-second. Due to advanced modulation of baud cycles as well as data compression, this is no longer true.

Beep codes A series of audible tones produced by a motherboard during the POST. These tones identify whether the POST has completed successfully or whether some piece of system hardware is not working properly. Consult the manual for your particular motherboard for a specific list of beep codes.

Binary numbers   A number system with a base of 2, unlike the number systems most of us use which have bases of 10 (decimal numbers), 12 (measurement in feet and inches), and 60 (time). Binary numbers are preferred for computers for precision and economy. An electronic circuit that can detect the difference between two states (on-off, 0-1) is easier and more inexpensive to build than one that could detect the differences among ten states (0–9).

BIOS (Basic Input/Output Services)   Classically, the software routines burned onto the System ROM of a PC. More commonly seen as any software that directly controls a particular piece of hardware. A set of programs encoded in Read-Only Memory (ROM) on computers. These programs handle startup operations and low-level control of hardware such as disk drives, the keyboard, and monitor.

Bit (binary digit)   A bit is a single binary digit. Any device that can be in an on or off state.

Bit depth   The number of colors a video card is capable of producing. Common bit depths are 16-bit and 32-bit, representing 65,536 colors and 16.7 million colors respectively.

Bootable disk   A disk that contains a functional operating system; can also be a floppy disk or CD-ROM.

Bootstrap loader   Lines of code in a system's BIOS that scan for an operating system; looks specifically for a valid boot sector and when one is found, control is handed over to boot sector and bootstrap loader removes itself from memory.

BPS (bits per second)   Measurement of how fast data is moved from one place to another. A 56K modem can move 56,000 bits per second.

Buffer underrun   The inability of a source device to provide a CD-burner with a constant stream of data while burning a CD-R or CD-RW.

Bus   A series of wires connecting two or more separate electronic devices that enable those devices to communicate.

Bus topology   A configuration wherein all computers connect to the network via a central bus cable.

Byte   Eight contiguous bits, the fundamental data unit of personal computers. Storing the equivalent of one character, the byte is also the basic unit of measurement for computer storage. Bytes are counted in powers of two.

C

Cache   A special area of RAM that stores the data most frequently accessed from the hard drive. Cache memory can optimize the use of your systems.

Cache memory   A special section of fast memory chips set aside to store the information most frequently accessed from RAM.

Caching   The act of holding data in cache memory for faster access and use.

Card services   The uppermost level of PCMCIA services. The card services level recognizes the function of a particular PC Card and provides the specialized drivers necessary to make the card work.

CardBus   32-bit PC cards that can support up to eight (8) devices on each card. Electrically incompatible with earlier PC cards (3.3V versus 5V).

Catastrophic failure   Occurs when a component or whole system will not boot; usually related to manufacturing defect of a component. Could also be caused by overheating and physical damage to computer components.

Cathode ray tube (CRT)   The tube of a monitor in which rays of electrons are beamed onto a phosphorescent screen to produce images. Also a shorthand way to describe a monitor that uses CRT rather than LCD technology.

CD quality   CD quality audio has a sample rate of 44.4 KHz and a bit rate of 128-bits.

CD-DA (CD-Digital Audio)   A special format used for early CD-ROMs and all audio CDs; divides data into variable length tracks. A good format to use for audio tracks but terrible for data due to lack of error checking.

CD-R (Compact Disk Recordable)   A type of CD technology that accepts a single "burn" but cannot be erased after that one burn.

CD-ROM (Compact Disk Read-Only Memory)   A read-only compact storage disk for audio or video data. Recordable devices, such as CD-Rs, are updated versions of the older CD-ROM players. CD-ROMs are read using *CD-ROM drives.*

CD-RW (Compact Disk Read/Write)   A type of CD technology that accepts multiple reads/writes like a hard drive.

Centronics connector   A type of connector commonly used with printers and SCSI-1 devices, distinguished by a central contact board rather than pins, and secured in place by clips.

Chipset   Electronic chips that handle all of the low-level functions of a PC, which in the original PC were handled by close to 30 different chips. Chipsets usually consist of one, two, or three separate chips embedded into a motherboard to handle all of these functions.

Cleaning kit   A set of tools used to clean a device or piece of media.

Clock   An electronic circuit utilizing a quartz crystal that generates evenly spaced pulses at speeds of millions of cycles per second. The pulses are used to synchronize the flow of information through the computer's internal communication channels. Some computers also contain a circuit that tracks hours, minutes, and seconds.

Clock cycle   A single charge to the clock wire of a CPU.

Clock multiplying CPU   A CPU that takes the incoming clock signal and multiples it inside the CPU to let the internal circuitry of the CPU run faster.

Clock speed   The speed at which a CPU executes instructions, measured in MHz or GHz. In modern CPUs, the internal speed is general a multiple of the external speed. *See also* Clock multiplying CPU.

CMOS (Complimentary Metal-Oxide Semiconductor) Originally, the type of non-volatile RAM that held information about the most basic parts of your PC such as hard drives, floppies, and amount of DRAM. Today, actual CMOS chips have been replaced by Flash-type non-volatile RAM. The information is the same, however, and is still called CMOS—even though it is now almost always stored on Flash RAM.

Coaxial cable Cabling in which an internal conductor is surrounded by another, outer conductor, thus sharing the same axis.

Codec (Compressor/Decompressor) Software that compresses or decompresses media streams.

COM port(s) A system name that refers to the serial communications ports available on your computer. When used as a program extension, .COM indicates an executable program file limited to 64K.

Common command set (CCS) A set of 18 commands introduced with SCSI-2 devices that made installing and configuring SCSI devices much easier.

Component failure Occurs when a system device fails due to manufacturing or some other type of defect.

Conditioning charger A battery charger that contains intelligent circuitry that prevents portable computer batteries from being overcharged and damaged.

CONFIG.SYS An ASCII text file in the root directory that contains configuration commands. CONFIG.SYS enables the system to be set up to configure high, expanded, and extended memories by the loading of HIMEM.SYS and EMM386.EXE drivers, as well as drivers for non-standard peripheral components.

Connectors Used to attach cables to a system. Common types of connectors include USB, PS/2, and DB-25.

Convergence A measure of how sharply a single pixel appears on a CRT; a monitor with poor convergence would produce images that are not sharply defined.

CPU (Central Processing Unit) The "brain" of the computer. The microprocessor that handles the primary calculations for the computer. They are known by names such as Pentium 4 and Athlon.

CRIMM (Continuity RIMM) A passive device added to populate unused banks in a system that uses RAMBUS RIMMs.

D

Daisy-chaining A method of connecting together several devices along a bus and managing the signals for each device.

DB connectors D-shaped connectors used for a variety of connections in the PC and networking world. Can be male (with prongs) or female (with holes) and have a varying number of pins or sockets.

DB-25 connector DB connector (female), commonly referred to as a parallel port connector.

Decoder   A tool used to decode data that has been encoded; for instance, a DVD decoder breaks down the code used to encrypt the data on a piece of DVD Video media.

Degauss   The procedure used to break up the electromagnetic fields that can build up on the cathode ray tube of a monitor; involves running a current through a wire loop. Most monitors feature a manual degaussing tool.

Desktop extender   A type of portable computer that offers some of the features of a full-fledged desktop computer, but with a much smaller footprint and lower weight.

Desktop replacement   A type of portable computer that offers the same performance of a full-fledged desktop computer; these systems are normally very heavy to carry and often cost much more than the desktop systems they replace.

Device driver   A subprogram to control communications between the computer and peripherals.

Digital Theatre Systems (DTS)   A technology for sound reductions and channeling methods, similar to Dolby Digital.

Direct current (DC)   A type of electricity where the flow of electrons is in a complete circle.

DirectSound3D (DS3D)   Introduced with DirectX 3.0, DS3D is a command set used to create positional audio, or sounds that appear to come from in front, in back, or to the side of a user. *See also* DirectX.

DirectX   A series of standards promulgated by Microsoft that enables applications running on Windows platforms to control hardware directly.

Disk thrashing   A term used to describe a hard disk drive that is constantly being accessed due to the lack of available system memory. When system memory runs low, a Windows system will utilize hard disk space as "virtual" memory, thus causing the unusual amount of hard disk drive access.

Display adapter   *See* Video card.

DMA (Direct Memory Access)   A technique that some PC hardware devices use to transfer data to and from the memory without using the CPU.

Docking station   A docking station is a box with additional ports and drives to which you attach a portable PC. Most docking stations use a proprietary connector. Often confused with a *port replicator*, a similar device that lacks extra drives.

Dolby Digital   A technology for sound reductions and channeling methods.

Dot-matrix printer   A printer that creates each character from an array of dots. Pins striking a ribbon against the paper, one pin for each dot position, form the dots. The printer may be a serial printer (printing one character at a time) or a line printer.

Dot pitch   A value relating to CRTs, showing the diagonal distance between phosphors measured in millimeters.

Double Data Rate SDRAM (DDR SDRAM)   A type of DRAM that makes two processes for every clock cycle. *See also* DRAM.

Double-sided double density   A type of floppy disk that is capable of holding 360 KB on a 5.25-inch disk and 720 KB of data of 3.5-inch disk. This format can be read in all modern floppy disk drives.

Double-sided high density   A type of floppy disk that is capable of holding 1.2 MB on a 5.25-inch disk and 1.44 MB on a 3.5-inch disk. This format can be read in all modern floppy disk drives.

DPI (dots per inch)   A measure of printer resolution that counts the dots the device can produce per linear (horizontal) inch.

DRAM (Dynamic Random Access Memory or Dynamic RAM)   The memory used to store data in most personal computers. DRAM stores each bit in a "cell" composed of a transistor and a capacitor. Because the capacitor in a DRAM cell can only hold a charge for a few milliseconds, DRAM must be continually refreshed, or rewritten, to retain its data.

Drive change signal   A signal created by a floppy disk drive when a floppy disk is inserted into the drive; transmitted on the 34th wire in a floppy disk drive cable. When Windows first reads a floppy disk, the directory is stored in RAM until the drive change signal indicates that the disk has been removed or that data has been changed.

DSL (Digital Subscriber Line)   A high-speed Internet connection technology that uses a regular telephone line for connectivity. DSL comes in several varieties, including Asynchronous (ADSL) and Synchronous (SDSL), and many speeds. Typical home-user DSL connections are ADSL with a download speed of up to 1.5 Mbps and an upload speed of 384 Kbps.

Dual Inline Memory Module (DIMM)   A type of DRAM packaging, similar to SIMMs with the distinction that each side of each tab inserted into the system performs a separate function. Comes in a compact 72-pin SO DIMM format, and full-size 144- and 168-pin formats. This 64-bit memory module is currently the standard memory package on modern computers. Types of DIMMs include SDRAM and DDR SDRAM.

Dual Inline Pin Package (DIPP)   An early type of RAM package that featured two rows of exposed connecting pins; very fragile and difficult to install. DIPPs were replaced first with SIPPs and later with SIMMs and DIMMs.

DVD (Digital Versatile Disk)   A CD media format that provides for 4–17 GB of video or data storage.

DVD Multi   A description given to DVD drives that are capable of reading all six DVD formats.

DVD+RW   A type of rewriteable DVD media.

DVD-ROM   The DVD-ROM is the DVD equivalent of the standard CD-ROM.

DVD-RW   A type of rewriteable DVD media.

DVD-Video   A DVD format used exclusively to store digital video; capable of storing more than two hours of high-quality video on a single DVD.

E

EAX   3-D sound technology developed by Creative Labs, but now supported by most sound cards.

EDB (external data bus)   The primary data highway of all computers. Everything in your computer is tied either directly or indirectly to the external data bus. *See also* Frontside bus and Backside bus.

EDO (Enhanced Data Out) DRAM   An improvement on FPM DRAM in that more data can be read before the RAM must be refreshed.

EISA (Enhanced ISA)   An improved expansion bus, based on the ISA bus, with a top speed of 8.33 MHz, a 32-bit data path, and a high degree of self-configuration. Backwardly compatible with legacy ISA cards.

Error correction code (ECC) DRAM   A type of RAM that uses special chips to detect and fix memory errors. This type of RAM is commonly used in high-end servers where data integrity is crucial.

Ethernet   Name coined by Xerox for the first standard of network cabling and protocols. Ethernet is based on a bus topology.

Expansion bus   Set of wires going to the CPU, governed by the expansion bus crystal, directly connected to expansion slots of varying types (ISA, PCI, AGP, etc.). Depending on the type of slots, the expansion bus runs at a percentage of the main system speed (8.33–66 MHz).

Expansion bus crystal   A crystal, originally designed by IBM, which controls the speed of the expansion bus.

Expansion slots   1. Connectors on a motherboard that allow a user to add optional components to a system. *See also* AGP (Accelerated Graphics Port) and PCI (Peripheral Component Interconnect). 2. A receptacle connected to the computer's expansion bus, designed to accept adapters.

External data bus (EDB)   The primary data highway of all computers. Everything in your computer is tied either directly or indirectly to the external data bus. *See also* Frontside bus and Backside bus.

F

FireWire (1394)   An IEEE 1394 standard to send wide-band signals over a thin connector system that plugs into TVs, VCRs, TV cameras, PCs, etc. This serial bus developed by Apple and Texas Instruments enables connection of 60 devices at speeds ranging from 100 to 400 megabits per second.

Firmware   Embedded programs or code that is stored on a ROM chip. Firmware is generally OS-independent, thus allowing devices to operate in a wide variety of circumstances without direct OS support.

Flash ROM   A type of ROM technology that can be electrically reprogrammed while still in the PC. Flash is overwhelmingly the most common storage medium of BIOS in PCs today, as it can be upgraded without even having to open the computer on most systems.

FlexATX   A motherboard form factor. Motherboards built in accordance with the FlexATX form factor are very small, much smaller than microATX motherboards.

Flexing   Flexing is caused when components are installed on a motherboard after it has been installed into a computer case. Excessive flexing can cause damage to the motherboard itself.

Floppy disk   A type of removable storage media that can hold between 720 KB and 1.44 MB of data.

Floppy drive   A piece of system hardware that uses removable 3.5-inch disks as storage media.

FM synthesis   A method for producing sound that used electronic emulation of various instruments to more or less produce music and other sound effects.

Forced perfect termination (FPT)   A method for terminating SCSI devices that uses diodes instead of resistors.

Form factor   A standard for the physical organization of motherboard components and motherboard size. The most common form factors are ATX, NLX, and AT.

Formatting   The process of magnetically mapping a disk to provide a structure for storing data; can be done to any type of disk, including a floppy disk, hard disk, or other type of removable disk.

FPM (Fast Page Mode)   DRAM that uses a "paging" function to increase access speed and to lower production costs. Virtually all DRAMS are FPM DRAM. The name FPM is also used to describe older style, non-EDO DRAM.

Frontside bus   Name for the wires that connect the CPU to the main system RAM. Generally running at speeds of 66–133 MHz. Distinct from the Expansion bus and the Backside bus, though it shares wires with the former.

Fuel cells   A new type of power source that uses chemical reactions to produce electricity. Lightweight, compact, and stable, these devices are expected to replace batteries as the primary power source for portable PCs.

Fuser assembly   A mechanism, found in laser printers, that uses two rollers to fuse toner to paper during the print process.

G

Graphical device interface (GDI)   The portion of the Windows OS that supports graphical elements such as scroll bars, menus, icons, and the like.

H

Hard disk   *See* Hard drive.

Hard drive   A data-recording system using solid disks of magnetic material turning at high speeds to store and retrieve programs and data in a computer. Also called a *hard disk*.

Hardware protocol   A hardware protocol defines many aspects of a network, from the packet type to the cabling and connectors used.

Hibernation   A power management setting where all data from RAM is written to the hard drive before going to sleep. Upon waking up, all information is retrieved from the hard disk drive and returned to RAM.

High-voltage anode   A component in a CRT monitor. The high voltage anode has very high voltages of electricity flowing through it.

High Voltage Differential (HVD)   A rare type of SCSI device that uses two wires for each bit of information: one wire for data and one for the inverse of this data. The inverse signal takes the place of the ground wire in the single-ended cable. By taking the difference of the two signals, the device can reject the common-mode noise in the data stream.

Horizontal refresh rate (HRR)   The amount of time it takes for a CRT to draw one horizontal line of pixels on a display.

Host adapter   An expansion card that serves as a host to a particular device; for instance, you can install a SCSI host adapter into a system to allow for SCSI functionality even if SCSI hardware was not originally included with the machine.

HotSync (Synchronization)   A term used to describe the synchronizing of files between a PDA and a desktop computer. HotSync is the name of the synchronization program that is used by PalmOS-based PDAs.

Hub   An electronic device that sits at the center of a star topology network and provides a common point for the connection of network devices. In a 10BaseT Ethernet network, the hub contains the electronic equivalent of a properly terminated bus cable; in a Token Ring network, the hub contains the electronic equivalent of a ring.

I

I/O addressing   The process of using the address bus to talk to system devices.

I/O Controller Hub (ICH5)   The official name for the Southbridge chip found in Intel's 875P chipset for the Pentium 4.

IEEE 1284   A standard governing parallel communication. *See also* IEEE.

Image file   A bit-by-bit image of the data to be burned on the CD or DVD—from one file to an entire disc—stored as a single file on a hard drive. Image files are particularly handy when copying from CD to CD or DVD to DVD.

Impact printer   A type of printer that uses pins and inked ribbons to print text or images on a piece of paper. These printers are noisy, slow, and have very low print quality.

Inkjet printer   A type of printer that uses liquid ink, sprayed through a series of tiny jets, to print text or images on a piece of paper.

Interrupt   A suspension of a process, such as the execution of a computer program, caused by an event external to the computer and performed in such a way that the process can be resumed. Events of this kind include sensors monitoring laboratory equipment or a user pressing an interrupt key.

Interrupt request (IRQ)   IRQs are hardware lines over which devices can send interrupt signals to the microprocessor. When you add a new device to a PC, you sometimes need to set its IRQ number. This specifies which interrupt line the device may use. IRQ conflicts used to be a common problem when adding expansion boards, but the Plug-and-Play specification has removed this headache in most cases.

IP address   Also called **Internet Address**. The numeric address of a computer connected to the Internet. The IP address is made up of octets of 8-bit binary numbers that are translated into their shorthand numeric values. The IP address can be broken down into a network ID and a host ID.

IRQ steering   A technique used by the PCI bus to avoid conflict with legacy devices. The PCI bus appears to support classic IRQs for PCI cards, but uses dynamically assigned interrupt channels when the cards actually need to interrupt.

ISA (Industry Standard Architecture)   The Industry Standard Architecture design is found in the original IBM PC for the slots on the motherboard that allowed additional hardware to be connected to the computer's motherboard. An 8-bit, 8.33 MHz expansion bus was designed by IBM for its AT computer and released to the public domain. An improved 16-bit bus was also released to the public domain. Various other designs such as IBM's MicroChannel and EISA bus tried to improve on the design without much popularity. ISA only supports 8- and 16-bit data paths, so 32-bit alternatives such as PCI and AGP have become popular. Although ISA slots linger on most motherboards, they are on the way out, replaced by the newer 32-bit slots.

ISDN (Integrated Services Digital Network)   The CCITT (Comité Consutatif Internationale de Télégraphie et Téléphonie) standard that defines a digital method for communications to replace the current analog telephone system. ISDN is superior to telephone lines because it supports up to 128 Kbps transfer rate for sending information from computer to computer. It also allows data and voice to share a common phone line.

J

Joystick   A peripheral often used while playing computer games; originally intended as a multi-purpose input device.

Joule   A unit of measurement of energy. Surge suppressors are rated in the number of joules they can handle during an electrical surge or spike.

K

Keyboard   An input device. There are two common types of keyboards—those that use a mini-DIN (PS/2) connection and those that use a USB connection.

Kilohertz (KHz)   A unit of measure that equals a frequency of one thousand cycles per second.

L

Laser printer An electro-photographic printer in which a laser is used as the light source.

LCD (Liquid Crystal Display) A type of display commonly used on portable PCs. Display technology that relies on polarized light passing through a liquid medium rather than on electron beams striking a phosphorescent surface.

Legacy device Any device that is not Plug-and-Play compatible.

Lithium-Ion (Li-Ion) A type of battery commonly used in portable PCs. Li-Ion batteries don't suffer from the memory effects of NiCd batteries and provide much more power for a great length of time.

Logical Unit Numbers (LUNs) A specialized SCSI configuration that allows for multiple devices to share a single SCSI ID. This type of arrangement is found most commonly in high-end servers that have large hard disk arrays.

Low Voltage Differential (LVD) A type of differential SCSI. LVD SCSI requires less power than HVD and is compatible with existing SE SCSI controllers and devices. LVD devices can sense the type of SCSI and then work accordingly. If you plug an LVD device into an SE chain, it will act as an SE device. If you plug an LVD device into LVD, it will run as LVD. LVD SCSI chains can be up to 12 meters in length.

LPT port LPT (for line port or line printer) ports refer specifically to system resources assigned to parallel ports. LPT1 is the combination of I/O address 370 and IRQ7, for example, whereas LPT2 is I/O 270 and IRQ5. Most users and technicians refer to the 25-pin female parallel port found on older PCs as an LPT port. Also commonly referred to as a printer port.

M

MAC (Media Access Control) address Unique 48-bit address assigned to each network card. IEEE assigns blocks of possible addresses to various NIC manufacturers to help ensure that the address is always unique. The Data Link layer of the OSI model uses MAC addresses for locating machines.

MCA (MicroChannel) Expansion bus architecture developed by IBM as the (unsuccessful) successor to ISA. MCA had a full 32-bit design as well as being self-configuring.

MCH (Memory Controller Hub) Intel's name for the Northbridge chip in some of their chipsets.

MicroATX A variation of the ATX form factor. MicroATX motherboards are generally smaller than their ATX counterparts, but retain all the same functionality.

Microprocessor See **CPU**.

Microsoft CD-ROM Extensions (MSCDEX) This program takes the device name set up in the CD-ROM's device driver line in CONFIG.SYS and assigns it a drive letter, thus allowing for CD-ROM support in DOS.

MIDI (Musical Instrument Digital Interface) MIDI is a standard that describes the interface between a computer and a device for simulating musical instruments. Rather than sending large sound samples, a computer can simply send "instructions" to the instrument describing pitch, tone, and duration of a sound. MIDI files are therefore very efficient. Because a MIDI file is made up of a set of instructions rather than a copy of the sound, it is easy to modify each component of the file. Additionally, it is possible to program many channels, or "voices," of music to be played simultaneously, creating symphonic sound.

Mini power connector A type of connector used to provide power to floppy disk drives.

Mobile CPU A CPU designed for use in portable computers that uses much less power than a normal, desktop CPU.

Modem (MOdulator/DEModulator) A device that converts a digital bit stream into an analog signal (modulation) and converts incoming analog signals back into digital signals (demodulation). The analog communications channel is typically a telephone line and the analog signals are typically sounds.

Molex connector A type of computer power connector. CD-ROM drives, hard disk drives, and case fans all use this type of connector. A Molex connector is keyed to prevent it from being inserted into a power port improperly.

Motherboard A flat piece of circuit board that resides inside your computer case. The motherboard has a number of connectors on it; you can use these connectors to attach a variety of devices to your system, including hard disk drives, CD-ROM drives, floppy disk drives, and sound cards.

Motherboard book A valuable resource when installing a new motherboard. The motherboard book normally lists all the specifications about a motherboard, including the type of memory and type of CPU that should be used with the motherboard.

Mouse An input device that allows a user to manipulate a cursor on the screen in order to select items.

MP3 Short for MPEG, Layer 3. MP3 is a type of compression used specifically for turning high-quality digital audio files into much smaller, yet similar sounding, files.

Multimedia Extensions (MMX) A set of specific CPU instructions that allows a CPU to handle many multimedia functions, such as digital signal processing. Introduced with the Pentium CPU, these instructions are now used on all x86 CPUs.

Multimeter A device that is used to measure voltage, amperage, and resistance.

MultiRead The ability of most modern CD-ROM drives to read a wide variety of discs is called Multi-Read. Modern CD-ROMs can read CD-ROM, CD-R, and CD-RW discs.

Multisession drive A recordable CD drive that is capable of burning multiple sessions on to a single recordable disc. A multisession drive also has the ability to "close" a CD-R so that no further tracks can be written to it.

N

Network Operating System (NOS)   An NOS is an operating system that provides basic file and supervisory services over a network. While each computer attached to the network will have its own OS, the NOS describes which actions are allowed by each user and coordinates distribution of networked files to the user who requests them.

NIC (Network Interface Card)   An expansion card that enables a PC to physically link to a network.

Nickel-Cadmium (Ni-Cd)   A type of battery that was used in the first portable PCs. Heavy and inefficient, these batteries also suffered from a memory effect that could drastically shorten the overall life of the battery. *See also* Nickel-Metal Hydride (Ni-MH), Lithium-Ion (Li-Ion).

Nickel-Metal Hydride (Ni-MH)   A type of battery used in portable PCs. Ni-MH batteries had fewer issues with the memory effect than Ni-Cd batteries. Ni-MH batteries have been replaced by Lithium-Ion batteries. *See also* Nickel-Cadmium (Ni-Cd), Lithium-Ion (Li-Ion).

Nit   A value used to measure the brightness of an LCD display. A typical LCD display has a brightness of between 100 and 400 nits.

Non-system disk or disk error   An error that occurs during the boot process. Common causes for this error are leaving a non-bootable floppy disk in the floppy disk drive while the computer is booting.

Non-volatile   A type of memory that retains data even if power is removed.

Northbridge   The Northbridge is the chip or chips that connect a CPU to memory, the PCI bus, Level 2 cache and AGP activities. The Northbridge chips communicate with the CPU through the FSB.

NVIDIA   A company that is one of the foremost manufacturers of graphics cards and chipsets.

O

Ohm(s)   Electronic measurement of a cable's impedance.

Online uninterruptible power supply (UPS)   An online UPS uses capacitors to store electricity and supply electricity for the PC directly. The AC from the wall socket only recharges the capacitors. As an added benefit, most online UPSs *condition* the electricity for the PC, providing a smooth, constant flow.

P

P1 connector   A type of connector used to provide power to ATX motherboards.

P4 12V connector   A type of connector used to provide additional 12v power to motherboards that support Pentium IV processors.

P8 and P9 connectors   A type of connector used to provide power to AT-style motherboards.

Packets   Small data units sent across a network.

Pages per minute (ppm)   A measure of the speed of a printer.

Parallel port   A connection for the synchronous, high-speed flow of data along parallel lines to a device, usually a printer.

Parity   A method of error detection where a small group of bits being transferred are compared to a single "parity" bit that is set to make the total bits odd or even. The receiving device reads the parity bit and determines if the data is valid based on the oddness or evenness of the parity bit.

PCI (Peripheral Component Interconnect)   A design architecture for the sockets on the computer motherboard that enable system components to be added to the computer. PCI is a "local bus" standard, meaning that devices added to a computer through this port will use the processor at the motherboard's full speed (up to 33 MHz), rather than at the slower 8 MHz speed of the regular bus. In addition to moving data at a faster rate, PCI moves data 32 or 64 bits at a time, rather than the 8 or 16 bits that the older ISA buses supported.

PCMCIA (Personal Computer Memory Card International Association)   Also called **PC Card**. A consortium of computer manufacturers who devised the standard for credit card-sized adapter cards that add functionality in many notebook computers, PDAs, and other computer devices. The simpler term "PC Card" has become more common in referring to these cards.

PDA (Personal Digital Assistant)   A handheld computer that blurs the line between the calculator and computer. Earlier PDAs were calculators that enabled the user to program in such information as addresses and appointments. Newer machines, such as the Palm Pilot, are fully programmable computers. Most PDAs use a pen/stylus for input rather than a keyboard. A few of the larger PDAs have a tiny keyboard in addition to the stylus.

Photo-CD   A compressed image format developed by Kodak that allows for many photos to be stored on a single CD-ROM.

Photosensitive drum   An aluminum cylinder coated with particles of photosensitive compounds that is used in a laser printer. The photosensitive drum is usually contained within the toner cartridge.

Pin 1   A designator used to ensure proper alignment of floppy disk drive and hard disk drive connectors.

Pin Grid Array (PGA)   A popular CPU package where a CPU is packaged in a ceramic material and a large number of pins extend from the bottom of the package in a regular pattern or array.

Ping (Packet Internet Groper)   Slang term for a small network message (ICMP ECHO) sent by a computer to check for the presence and aliveness of another. Also used to verify the presence of another system.

Pipeline   A processing methodology where multiple calculations take place simultaneously by being broken into a series of steps. Often used in CPUs and video processors.

Pixel (picture element)   In computer graphics, the smallest element of a display space that can be independently assigned color or intensity.

Plug and Play   Also called **PnP**. A combination of smart PCs, smart devices, and smart operating systems that automatically configure all the necessary system resources and ports when you install a new peripheral device.

Port   That portion of a computer through which a peripheral device may communicate. Often identified with the various plug-in jacks on the back of your computer. On a network hub, it is the connector that receives the wire link from a node.

Port replicator   A device that plugs into a USB port or other specialized port that offers common PC ports, such as serial, parallel, USB, network, and PS/2. By plugging your notebook computer into the port replicator, you can instantly connect it to non-portable components such as a printer, scanner, monitor, or a full- sized keyboard. Port replicators are typically used at home or in the office with the non-portable equipment already connected.

POST cards   A diagnostic tool used to identify problems that occur during the POST. These cards usually fit into a PCI slot and have a series of LED indicators to indicate any problems that occur during the POST. *See also* Power-On Self Test (POST).

PostScript   A language defined by Adobe Systems, Inc. for describing how to create an image on a page. The description is independent of the resolution of the device that will actually create the image. It includes a technology for defining the shape of a font and creating a raster image at many different resolutions and sizes.

Power supply   A device that provides the electrical power for a PC. A power supply converts the 110-volt AC power into usable types of DC electricity in a PC.

Power supply fan   A small fan located in a system power supply that draws warm air from inside the power supply and exhausts it to the outside.

Power-On Self Test (POST)   A basic diagnostic routine completed by a system at the beginning of the boot process. The POST checks to make sure that a display adapter is installed, that a system's memory is installed, and then searches for an operating system before handing over control of the machine to an operating system, if one is found.

PPP (Point-to-Point Protocol)   A protocol that enables a computer to connect to the Internet through a dial-in connection and enjoy most of the benefits of a direct connection. PPP is considered to be superior to SLIP because of its error detection and data compression features, which SLIP lacks, and the ability to use dynamic IP addresses.

Primary corona   A wire, located near the photosensitive drum in a laser printer, that is charged with extremely high voltage in order to form an electric field, enabling voltage to pass to the photosensitive drum, thus charging the photosensitive particles on the surface of the drum.

Print resolution   The number of pixels per inch of a print image.

Printer   An output device that can print text or illustrations on paper.

Printer Control Language (PCL) Hewlett-Packard's proprietary command set for controlling print jobs on printers.

R

Radial misalignment A term used to describe misaligned read/ write heads in a floppy disk drive.

RAM (Random Access Memory) Memory that can be accessed at random, that is, in which any memory address can be written to or read from without touching the preceding address. This term is often used to mean a computer's main memory.

Rambus DRAM (RDRAM) A patented RAM technology that uses accelerated clocks to provide very high-speed memory.

RAMDAC (Random Access Memory Digital-to-Analog Converter) Converts digital signals from the CPU and video processor into analog signals that the monitor can understand and thus draw the computer display properly. The RAMDAC speed is measured in MHz; higher speed can handle higher refresh rates.

REGEDIT.EXE A program used to edit the Windows registry.

REGEDT32.EXE A program used to edit the Windows registry. REGEDT32.EXE is available in Windows 2000 and XP only.

Registers Tiny temporary storage areas inside the CPU, used by the microprocessor to process complex commands. Modern registers come in 64- and 128-bit sizes.

Registry A complex binary file used to store configuration data about a particular system. To edit the Registry, a user can use the applets found in the Control Panel or REGEDIT.EXE or REGEDT32.EXE.

Resolution A measurement for CRTs and printers expressed in horizontal and vertical dots or pixels. Higher resolutions provide sharper details and thus display better-looking images.

RIMM (not an abbreviation) An individual stick of Rambus RAM.

Riser card A special adapter card, usually inserted into a special slot on a motherboard, that changes the orientation of expansion cards relative to the motherboard. Riser cards are extensively in slimline computers in order to keep total depth and height of the system to a minimum.

RJ (Registered Jack) UTP cable connectors, used for both telephone and network connections. **RJ-11** is a connector for four-wire UTP; usually found in telephone connections. **RJ-45** is a connector for eight-wire UTP; usually found in network connections and used for 10BaseT and 100BaseT networking.

ROM (Read-Only Memory) The generic term for non-volatile memory that can be read from but not written to. This means that code and data stored in ROM cannot be corrupted by accidental erasure. Additionally, ROM retains its data when power is removed, which makes it the perfect medium for storing BIOS data or information such as scientific constants.

S

Sampling   The process of capturing sound waves in electronic format.

SCSI (Small Computer System Interface)   A powerful and flexible peripheral interface popularized on the Macintosh and used to connect hard drives, CD-ROM drives, tape drives, scanners, and other devices to PCs of all kinds. Because SCSI is less efficient at handling small drives than IDE, it did not become popular on IBM-compatible computers until price reductions made these large drives affordable. Normal SCSI enables up to seven devices to be connected through a single bus connection, whereas Wide SCSI can handle 15 devices attached to a single controller.

SCSI chain   A series of SCSI devices working together through a host adapter.

SCSI ID   A unique identifier used by SCSI devices. No two SCSI devices may have the same SCSI ID.

SCSI-1   The first official SCSI standard. SCSI-1 is defined as an 8-bit, 5 MHz bus capable of supporting eight SCSI devices.

SCSI-2   Another SCSI standard that was the first SCSI standard to address all aspects of SCSI in detail. SCSI-2 defined a common command set that allowed all SCSI devices to communicate with one another.

SCSI-3   The latest SCSI standard that offers transfer rates up to 320 Mbps.

Sector   A segment of one of the concentric tracks encoded on the disk during a low-level format. Sectors hold 512 bytes on data.

Serial-Attached SCSI (SAS)   A serial version of SCSI. The industry's response to Serial ATA, SAS is a point-to-point interface that uses a reduced-size data cable and has reduced power consumption demands.

Serial port   A common connector on a PC, used connecting input devices (such as a mouse) or communications devices (such as a modem).

Single Edge Cartridge (SEC)   A radical CPU package where the CPU was contained in a cartridge that snapped into a special slot on the motherboard called *Slot 1*.

Single Inline Memory Module (SIMM)   A type of DRAM packaging distinguished by having a number of small tabs that install into a special connector. Each side of each tab is the same signal. SIMMs come in two common sizes: 30-pin and 72-pin.

Single Inline Pin Package (SIPP)   An early memory package that was the first to have individual RAM chips soldered onto small boards which were inserted into sockets on a motherboard. SIPPs were delicate, however, due to the exposed pins that were inserted into the motherboard connectors.

Single-ended (SE)   A term used to describe SCSI-1 devices that used only one wire to communicate a single bit of information. Single-ended SCSI devices are vulnerable to common-mode noise when used in conjunction with SCSI cables over 6 meters in length.

Single-session drive   An early type of CD-R drive that required a disc to be burned in a single session. This type of drives has been replaced by multisession drives. *See also* Multisession drive.

Slimline   A motherboard form factor used to create PCs that were very thin. NLX and LPX were two examples of this form factor.

Slot covers   Metal plates that cover up unused expansion slots on the back of a PC. These items are useful in maintaining proper airflow through a computer case.

Small Outline DIMM (SO DIMM)   A type of memory used in portable PCs because of its small size. SO DIMMs commonly have 72-, 144-, or 200-pins.

Smart Battery   A new type of portable PC battery that tells the computer when it needs to be charged, conditioned, or replaced.

SMM (System Management Mode)   A special CPU mode that enables the CPU to reduce power consumption via the selective shutdown of peripherals.

Socket   A combination of a port number and an IP address that uniquely identifies a connection. Also a mounting area for an electronic chip.

Socket services   Device drivers that support the PC Card socket, enabling the system to detect when a PC Card has been inserted or removed, and providing the necessary I/O to the device.

Soft-off by PWRBTN   A value found in the BIOS of most ATX motherboards. This value controls the length of time that the power button must be depressed in order for an ATX computer to turn off. If the on/off switch is set for a four-second delay, you must hold down the switch for four seconds before the computer cuts off.

Soft power   A characteristic of ATX motherboards. They can use software to turn the PC on and off. The physical manifestation of soft power is the power switch. Instead of the thick power cord used in AT systems, an ATX power switch is little more than a pair of small wires leading to the motherboard.

Sony/Philips digital interface (SPDIF)   A digital audio connector found on many high-end sound cards. This connector allows a user to connect their computer directly to a 5.1 speaker system or receiver.

Sound card   An expansion card that can produce audible tones when connected to a set of speakers.

Sounds and audio devices   A Control Panel applet used to configure audio hardware and software in Windows XP.

Southbridge   The Southbridge is part of a motherboard chipset. It handles all the inputs and outputs to the many devices in the PC.

SPS (Stand-by Power Supply or System)   A device that supplies continuous clean power to a computer system immediately following a power failure. *See also* UPS.

SRAM (Static RAM)   A type of RAM that uses a flip-flop type circuit rather than the typical transistor/capacitor of DRAM to hold a bit of information. SRAM does not need to be refreshed and is faster than regular DRAM. Used primarily for cache.

Standouts   Small connectors that screw into a computer case. A motherboard is then placed on top of the standouts and small screws are used to secure the motherboard to the standouts.

STP (Shielded Twisted Pair)   A popular cabling for networks composed of pairs of wires twisted around each other at specific intervals. The twists serve to reduce interference (also called *crosstalk*). The more twists, the less interference. The cable has metallic shielding to protect the wires from external interference. Token Ring networks are the only common network technology that uses STP, although Token Ring more often now uses UTP.

Subnet mask   The value used in TCP/IP settings to divide the IP address of a host into its component parts: network ID and host ID.

Subwoofer   A large, powerful speaker capable of producing extremely low frequency sounds.

Super I/O chip   A chip found on modern motherboards that provides legacy support.

Super video graphics array (SVGA)   Any display mode that goes beyond VGA (640 ? 480 at 16 colors) in either resolution or color depth can be labeled as SVGA, or Super VGA.

Surge suppressor   An inexpensive device that protects your computer from voltage spikes.

Synchronous DRAM (SDRAM)   A type of DRAM that is synchronous, or tied to the system clock. This type of RAM is used in all modern systems.

System BIOS   The primary set of BIOS stored on an EPROM or Flash chip on the motherboard. Defines the BIOS for all the assumed hardware on the motherboard, such as keyboard controller, floppy drive, basic video, RAM, etc.

System resources   System resources are I/O addresses, IRQs, DMA channels, and memory addresses.

SYSTEM.INI   An early Windows 3.*x* configuration file used to load device drivers. Windows 9*x*/Me systems require this file or they will not boot. Windows 2000 and XP systems do not require this file, but often have a copy in order to maintain backward compatibility with older Windows applications.

T

TCP/IP (Transmission Control Protocol/Internet Protocol)   A set of communication protocols developed by the U.S. Department of Defense that enables dissimilar computers to share information over a network.

TCP/IP services   A set of special sharing functions unique to TCP/IP. The most famous is Hypertext Transfer Protocol (HTTP), the language of the World Wide Web. Telnet and Ping are two other widely used TCP/IP services.

Termination   The use of terminating resistors to prevent packet reflection on a network cable.

Thin film transistor (TFT)   A type of LCD screen. *See also* Active Matrix.

Token Ring   A LAN and protocol in which nodes are connected together in a ring; a special packet called a *token* passed from node to node around the ring controls communication. A node can send data only when it receives the token and the token is not in use. This avoids the collision problems endemic to Ethernet networks.

Toner The toner in a laser printer is a fine powder made up of plastic particles bonded to iron particles, used to create the text and images during the printing process.

Toner cartridge The object used to store the toner in a laser printer. *See also* Laser printer, Toner.

Touchpad A flat, touch-sensitive pad just in front of the keyboard. To operate a touchpad, you glide your finger across its surface to move the pointer, and tap the surface once or twice to single- or double-click.

Traces Small electrical connections embedded in a circuit board.

Transfer corona A thin wire, usually protected by other thin wires, which applies a positive charge to the paper during the laser printing process, drawing the negatively charged toner particles off of the drum and onto the paper.

Triad A group of three phosphors—red, green, blue—in a CRT.

U

UART (Universal Asynchronous Receiver/Transmitter) A UART is a device that turns serial data into parallel data. The cornerstone of serial ports and modems.

UPS (uninterruptible power supply) A device that supplies continuous clean power to a computer system the whole time the computer is on. Protects against power outages and sags. The term UPS is often used mistakenly when people mean SPS (Stand-by Power Supply).

USB (universal serial bus) A 12 Mbps serial interconnect for keyboards, printers, joysticks, and many other devices. Enables hot-swapping and daisy chaining devices.

UTP (Unshielded Twisted Pair) A popular type of cabling for telephone and networks, composed of pairs of wires twisted around each other at specific intervals. The twists serve to reduce interference (also called *crosstalk*). The more twists, the less interference. The cable has *no* metallic shielding to protect the wires from external interference, unlike its cousin, STP. 10BaseT uses UTP, as do many other networking technologies. UTP is available in a variety of grades, called *categories*, as defined here:

Category 1 UTP	Regular analog phone lines—not used for data communications.
Category 2 UTP	Supports speeds up to 4 megabits per second.
Category 3 UTP	Supports speeds up to 16 megabits per second. Minimum cabling for 10BaseT.
Category 4 UTP	Supports speeds up to 20 megabits per second.
Category 5 UTP	Supports speeds up to 100 megabits per second. Minimum cabling for 100BaseT.
Category 5e UTP	Supports speeds up to 1 gigabit per second.
Category 6 UTP	Supports speeds up to 10 gigabits per second.

V

V standards   Standards established by CCITT for modem manufacturers to follow (voluntarily) to ensure compatible speeds, compression, and error correction.

Vertical refresh rate (VRR)   A measurement of the amount of time it takes for a CRT to completely draw a complete screen. This value is measured in Hertz, or cycles per second. Most modern CRTs have a VRR of 60 Hz or better.

VGA (Video Graphics Array)   The standard for the video graphics adapter that was built into IBM's PS/2 computer. It supports 16 colors in a 640 ? 480 pixel video display, and quickly replaced the older CGA (Color Graphics Adapter) and EGA (Extended Graphics Adapter) standards.

VIA Technologies   Major manufacturer of chipsets for motherboards. Also produces Socket 370 CPUs through its subsidiary Cyrix that compete directly with Intel.

Video card   An expansion card that works with the CPU to produce the images that are displayed on your computer's display.

Viewable image size (VIS)   A measurement of the viewable image that is displayed by a CRT rather than a measurement of the CRT itself.

VLB (VESA Local Bus)   VESA Local Bus is a design architecture for the sockets on the computer motherboard that enable system components to be added to the computer. VLB was the first "local bus" standard, meaning that devices added to a computer through this port would use the processor at its full speed, rather than at the slower 8 MHz speed of the regular bus. In addition to moving data at a faster rate, VLB moves data 32 bits at a time, rather than the 8 or 16 bits that the older ISA buses supported. Although common on machines using Intel's 486 CPU, modern computers now use PCI buses instead.

Voice coil motor   A type of motor used to spin hard disk drive platters.

Volts (V)   The pressure of the electrons passing through a wire is called voltage and is measured in units called volts (V).

W

Wattage (watts or W)   The amount of amps and volts needed by a particular device to function is expressed as how much wattage (watts or W) that device needs.

Wave table synthesis   A technique that supplanted FM synthesis, wherein recordings of actual instruments or other sounds are embedded in the sound card as WAV files. When a particular note from a particular instrument or voice is requested, the sound processor grabs the appropriate prerecorded WAV file from its memory and adjusts it to match the specific sound and timing requested.

Write Once Read Many (WORM)   Early CD technologies that allowed users to burn their own CD-ROMs, doomed by high equipment costs. Supplanted by CD-R technology.

Z

ZIF (zero insertion force) socket A socket for CPUs that enables insertion of a chip without much pressure. Intel promoted the ZIF socket with its overdrive upgrades. The chip is dropped into the socket's holes and a small lever is flipped to lock them in. Somewhat replaced in modern motherboards by Slot 1 and Slot A architecture, but still in style in Super Socket 7, Socket A, and Socket 370 motherboards.

Index

INTERNATIONAL CONTACT INFORMATION

AUSTRALIA
McGraw-Hill Book Company
Australia Pty. Ltd.
TEL +61-2-9900-1800
FAX +61-2-9878-8881
http://www.mcgraw-hill.com.au
books-it_sydney@mcgraw-hill.com

CANADA
McGraw-Hill Ryerson Ltd.
TEL +905-430-5000
FAX +905-430-5020
http://www.mcgraw-hill.ca

**GREECE, MIDDLE EAST, & AFRICA
(Excluding South Africa)**
McGraw-Hill Hellas
TEL +30-210-6560-990
TEL +30-210-6560-993
TEL +30-210-6560-994
FAX +30-210-6545-525

MEXICO (Also serving Latin America)
McGraw-Hill Interamericana Editores
S.A. de C.V.
TEL +525-1500-5108
FAX +525-117-1589
http://www.mcgraw-hill.com.mx
carlos_ruiz@mcgraw-hill.com

SINGAPORE (Serving Asia)
McGraw-Hill Book Company
TEL +65-6863-1580
FAX +65-6862-3354
http://www.mcgraw-hill.com.sg
mghasia@mcgraw-hill.com

SOUTH AFRICA
McGraw-Hill South Africa
TEL +27-11-622-7512
FAX +27-11-622-9045
robyn_swanepoel@mcgraw-hill.com

SPAIN
McGraw-Hill/
Interamericana de España, S.A.U.
TEL +34-91-180-3000
FAX +34-91-372-8513
http://www.mcgraw-hill.es
professional@mcgraw-hill.es

**UNITED KINGDOM, NORTHERN,
EASTERN, & CENTRAL EUROPE**
McGraw-Hill Education Europe
TEL +44-1-628-502500
FAX +44-1-628-770224
http://www.mcgraw-hill.co.uk
emea_queries@mcgraw-hill.com

ALL OTHER INQUIRIES Contact:
McGraw-Hill/Osborne
TEL +1-510-420-7700
FAX +1-510-420-7703
http://www.osborne.com
omg_international@mcgraw-hill.com

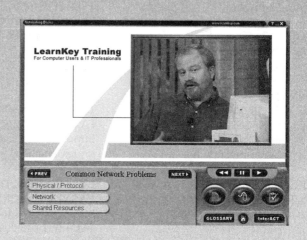

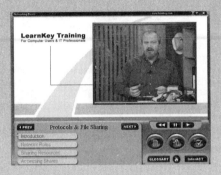

Sound Off!

Visit us at **www.osborne.com/bookregistration** and let us know what you thought of this book. While you're online you'll have the opportunity to register for newsletters and special offers from McGraw-Hill/Osborne.

We want to hear from you!

Sneak Peek

Visit us today at **www.betabooks.com** and see what's coming from McGraw-Hill/Osborne tomorrow!

Based on the successful software paradigm, Bet@Books™ allows computing professionals to view partial and sometimes complete text versions of selected titles online. Bet@Books™ viewing is free, invites comments and feedback, and allows you to "test drive" books in progress on the subjects that interest you the most.